*For all readers,
young and old(er)*

ULTIMATE FOOTBALL HEROES

Matt Oldfield is an accomplished writer and the editor-in-chief of football review site *Of Pitch & Page*. Tom Oldfield is a freelance sports writer and the author of biographies on Cristiano Ronaldo, Arsène Wenger and Rafael Nadal.

Cover illustration by Dan Leydon.
To learn more about Dan visit danleydon.com
To purchase his artwork visit etsy.com/shop/footynews
Or just follow him on Twitter @danleydon

South Dublin Libraries
www.southdublinlibraries.ie

TABLE OF CONTENTS

CHAPTER 1

EUROPEAN CHAMPION!

1 June 2019, Wanda Metropolitano Stadium, Madrid

'Right, lads,' Jordan Henderson called out from the front of the Liverpool line. 'It's time for us to go out there and win the Champions League!'

'YEAH!' the others cheered behind him. They couldn't lose in the final again – not for a second year in a row! The 3–1 defeat to Real Madrid in 2018 had been so disappointing, but Liverpool had bounced straight back, and this time, they were taking on a team they knew very well – their Premier League rivals, Tottenham.

One by one, the Liverpool players followed their

captain through the tunnel, past the gigantic, silver trophy, and onto the pitch:

Goalkeeper Alisson,

Defenders Joël Matip, Andy Robertson and Trent Alexander-Arnold,

Gini Wijnaldum, Virgil van Dijk, Fabinho,

And finally, the 'Fab Three', the team's star strikeforce:

Roberto Firmino, Mohamed Salah and Sadio Mané.

As Sadio looked up at the thousands of excited faces in the stadium, he could already hear the supporters singing their special song:

We've got Salah, do do do do do do!
Mané Mané, do do do do do,
And Bobby Firmino,
And we sold Coutinho!

The pressure was really on for them to perform, but that didn't bother Sadio. Yes, it was the biggest game of the year, but he was a big game player. He had shown it by scoring in the 2018 Champions

League Final, and on the last day of the 2018–19 Premier League season too. On both occasions, however, Liverpool had failed to lift the trophies they so desperately wanted. Now, in Madrid, Sadio didn't care about scoring; all he cared about was winning.

After beating Lionel Messi's Barcelona 4–3 in the 'Miracle of Anfield', it felt like 2019 *had* to be Liverpool's year to lift the Champions League again. It would be the first time since the 'Miracle of Istanbul' in 2005, which Sadio had watched on TV as a thirteen-year-old boy back in Bambali. But Tottenham, too, had pulled off an incredible semi-final comeback to edge past Ajax. In the final, there could only be one winner.

'And it's going to be Liverpool!' Sadio thought. He was absolutely sure of it.

He had done the Austrian Double with Red Bull Salzburg back in 2014, but since then? Nothing! Sadio was twenty-seven years old now and he couldn't wait any longer. He was determined to collect another winners' medal at last.

A strong start – that's what Liverpool needed, and

that's exactly what they got. After fifteen seconds,
Jordan lifted the ball over the Tottenham defence, for
Sadio to chase down the left wing…

ZOOM! With that sudden burst of speed, he was
away from Kieran Trippier in a flash.

'Go on,' the Liverpool fans urged, jumping out of
their seats. 'SHOOT!'

That was Sadio's first thought, but it took a little
while to control the bouncing ball. By then, the
shooting chance had gone, so what was his Plan
B? As he looked up, he spotted Jordan making a
late run into the box. But when he tried to chip a
pass through to him, it struck the Spurs midfielder
Moussa Sissoko on the arm.

'Handball!' Sadio screamed, raising his arm in
the referee's direction whereupon Damir Skomina
reacted and pointed to the spot. *Penalty!*

What a start – it was still only the first minute
of the match! Sadio gave the supporters the signal:
'Make more noise!'

Liverpool! Liverpool! Liverpool!

Another big game, another big game moment

from Sadio. He hadn't scored himself, but hopefully, he had helped his team to take a giant step towards victory...

Mohamed ran up and... scored. *1–0!*

'Come on!' As the other Liverpool players chased after their goalscorer, Sadio sank to his knees and punched the air. Winning any trophy meant so much to him, but especially the Champions League. It would be a childhood dream come true.

There was still a long way to go, however – over ninety minutes of football, in fact.

'Stay focused!' Liverpool's manager Jürgen Klopp called, as he clapped and cheered on the sidelines.

Liverpool expected Tottenham to fight back strongly, but instead, it was Liverpool who had the better goalscoring chances.

As Andy got the ball on the left wing, Sadio skipped between the Spurs centre-backs. He could see the cross coming towards him and he stretched out his right leg... but Hugo Lloris rushed out to make a brave catch.

'Oooohhhhhhh!' Sadio gasped. *So close!*

Would one goal be enough? With five minutes to go, sub striker Divock Origi finally scored that all-important second. As Sadio watched the ball cross the line, he jumped for joy. Game over; Liverpool were about to be crowned the new Champions of Europe!

Klopp took Sadio off in the ninetieth minute but seconds later, he rushed back onto the pitch to celebrate with his teammates. Virgil, Gini, Trent, Mohamed, Naby Keïta – it was hugs and tears all around!

'We did it,' Sadio cried out as if he still couldn't believe the words. 'We won THE CHAMPIONS LEAGUE!'

First came the winners' medal and then the gigantic, silver trophy. As Jordan lifted it high above his head, the sky was filled with fireworks and loud Liverpool cheers.

Hurraaaaaaaay!

Liverpool! Liverpool! Liverpool!

Campeones, Campeones, Olé! Olé! Olé!

It was easily the best day of Sadio's life so far. It felt

like the end of a long and incredible journey, from the dusty streets of Senegal all the way to European football's greatest stage, via adventures in France, Austria and England. Through it all, he had never given up on following his big football dream.

'And look at me now – it was all worth it!' Sadio told himself happily.

He was the top scorer in the Premier League and a European Champion at last. As Sadio walked and danced around the pitch with a Senegal flag wrapped around his shoulders, he couldn't stop smiling. Why? Well, many reasons, but at that moment, Sadio was just imagining the joyful scenes back home in Bambali.

CHAPTER 2

THE BOY FROM BAMBALI

Unfortunately, while little Sadio was growing up, there was no football pitch in Bambali, the fishing village where he lived.

It was the early 1990s and football was becoming a big deal in Senegal's capital city, Dakar, but not in the southern Sédhiou region. Not yet anyway. For now, the young footballers of Bambali played in the dusty streets instead, or on the banks of the Casamance River.

As long as they had space and a ball, the kids were ready to kick off.

Pass!

Shoot!

GOAL!

At the age of three, Sadio was still too young to join in, but that didn't stop him watching and waiting for his chance. He stood there on the side, with his eyes fixed on the football action in front of him. He was hooked already. It was all so exciting – the running, the shouting, the tackling, the fast feet moving the ball around as if by magic.

'I'll be one of those Bambali football boys soon!' Sadio told himself. Playing football was the only thing he really thought about, other than food.

The problem was that he was a quiet, shy child. If he wanted to play, he was going to have to speak up eventually.

First, however, Sadio wanted to make sure that he was ready for his dream football debut. After all, he didn't want to embarrass himself in front of the older kids by giving the ball away or missing an open goal!

So, he practised on his own, kicking whatever he could find, whenever he could find it, and wherever he went.

Sometimes, it was a football, sometimes it was a

tin can, and sometimes, it was a rock – but it was always something.

'Stop!' his sisters shouted at the sound of his constant kicking. 'That noise is so annoying.'

'No, I need to practise!'

At last, Sadio was ready to ask to become one of the Bambali football boys. As soon as he had said the words 'Can I play?', he wondered why he had waited so long. What a waste of precious football time!

'Sure, what's your name?'

'Sadio.'

'Everyone, this is Sadio. Issa, he's on your team. Right, let's play!'

For the first few minutes, Sadio chased around the street like he was late for school. He was so desperate for his first touch of the football.

'Here – pass!' he called out bravely.

When, at last, the ball came to him, his heart felt like it might burst out of his chest. He had imagined this moment so many times, and now it was really happening. He was playing proper football! So, what was he going to do next?

On the one hand, Sadio had been learning lots of cool new tricks. Wasn't this his chance to test them out against real defenders? But on the other hand, he was the new kid and he didn't want the others to think that he was a show-off. No, no one liked a show-off.

'One step at a time,' he told himself, playing a simple pass instead.

Day after day, Sadio grew in confidence and skill on the football streets of Bambali. He was still too shy to say much to his teammates, but once a game kicked off, it was like he suddenly came alive. He was everywhere; running, shouting, tackling, his fast feet moving the ball around as if by magic. When he dribbled forward, it was like he was dancing.

GOAL! GOAL! GOAL!

'Man, you're *really* good now!' Issa told Sadio one day and those words meant the world to him. His dream was to become the best player in Bambali... ever! There had been talented footballers in the village before, but never a *famous* footballer. Not yet anyway. It wouldn't be easy, but Sadio was determined to make his dream come true.

Sadio's parents were happy that their son had a hobby that he loved so much. It kept him out of trouble, and it was a good use for all of his youthful energy. After a full day of school and then football, he was too tired to even squabble with his sisters.

'Just don't forget about your homework,' his parents warned him sternly. 'Remember, education is the most important thing!'

'Yes, Mum! Yes, Dad!'

Little Sadio kept his promise, even though he wasn't very interested in studying. The only time he really looked forward to going to school was when they set up a football tournament. With the chance to win at his favourite sport, suddenly he was the perfect pupil!

'Yes, Sir!'

'Thank you, Miss!'

Sadio was already working hard towards his dream. One day, the boy from Bambali was going to be a famous footballer.

CHAPTER 3

2002: SUPER SENEGAL!

To achieve his great ambition, Sadio was going to
need football heroes to look up to, and not just
from far and distant lands such as Europe and South
America. No, he wanted to watch African superstars,
players who had come from places like Bambali!
That was the most inspiring thing for a little boy
with a big football dream.

Nigeria's Nwankwo Kanu was shining for
Arsenal, and Cameroon's Samuel Eto'o was scoring
goal after goal for Real Mallorca, but what about
Sadio's country, Senegal? The national team had still
never played at a World Cup tournament, and their

best performance at the Africa Cup of Nations was fourth place.

'We're rubbish,' Sadio glumly told his best friend Boubacar. 'Even Mali made it to the final once!'

The year 2002, however, was a special one for Senegal, and for young Sadio too. He was now ten years old, the perfect age to enjoy the surprise success of 'The Lions of Teranga'.

The year started with the Africa Cup of Nations in Mali, their neighbours and biggest rivals. There were high hopes for Senegal's new generation of players. Most of the squad now played in Ligue 1, France's top division, and some were even challenging for the title.

Sadio's number one hero was the Lens forward, El Hadji Diouf. He was a deadly dribbler and a great goalscorer too, and he had just won the African Footballer of the Year award. He was the first player from Senegal to ever win the prize.

'Come on, you Lions!' Sadio cheered as he watched the games on TV in Bambali. He didn't miss a single match.

Super Senegal beat Egypt.

Then Zambia.

And then the Democratic Republic of the Congo.

The excitement was building, all across the
country. Suddenly, Sadio and his friends were so
proud of their national team. There was no one in
the squad from their Sédhiou region, but that didn't
matter; they were all Senegalese. Now, when the
kids played football in the streets of Bambali, they
pretended to be their new national heroes.

'I'm Diouf today!' Sadio said straight away.

'Fine, I'll be Pape Bouba Diop.'

'Call me Diao – Salif Diao!'

When the semi-final against Nigeria went to extra-
time, some people feared that Senegal would be
knocked out. Not Sadio, though – he was full
of belief.

'Super Senegal are going all the way!' he declared
confidently.

And he was right. Diouf crossed to Diao and...
GOAL – 2–1!

'*HURRAAAAAAY!*' The village of Bambali let out

its loudest cheer yet. Everyone was there watching together, huddled around the TV. For the first time ever, Super Senegal were through to the final of the Africa Cup of Nations!

When the big day arrived, there was a party atmosphere in the village. All work stopped and there was music and dancing in the streets. Whether they won or lost, the Senegal players would return home as heroes. Their amazing achievement would go down in history.

'Come on, you Lions!' everyone cheered as the final kicked off – Super Senegal vs Eto'o's Cameroon.

Sadio was more nervous than most. He hated the idea of second place; he was desperate to see his country lift Africa's greatest trophy.

After 120 minutes without a goal, the match went to penalties. When Tony Sylva saved Cameroon's first spot-kick, Sadio breathed a big sigh of relief. *Phew*, surely Super Senegal would now go on and win it?

But no, because Amdy Faye missed.

And so did Diouf.

And so did their captain, Aliou Cissé!

Instead, Cameroon were the Champions of Africa again. Back in Bambali, the tears streamed down Sadio's face. His country had come so close to glory. Eventually, however, Sadio turned that heartbreak into hunger.

'Once I become a famous footballer,' he told his friends, 'I'm going to lead Super Senegal to the Africa Cup of Nations final again, and this time, we'll win it!'

It wasn't all bad news for the team of 2002. By reaching the final, they had qualified for... the World Cup! Yes, that's right, Super Senegal were about to make their debut at football's top international tournament in Japan and South Korea.

'Come on, you Lions!' the people of Bambali cheered as their first match kicked off against France, then the current World Champions.

Even Sadio was fearing the worst, but it turned out to be the best – and most nail-biting – ninety minutes of football he had ever watched. Super Senegal were... SUPER!

Diouf flicked a header goalwards... but Fabien Barthez caught it safely.

Ooooohhhhh!

Diouf dribbled down the right wing, past Marcel Desailly, and then pulled the ball back to Khalilou Fadiga… but his shot was saved again.

Aaaaahhhhh!

Then, in the thirtieth minute, Diouf dribbled down the left wing, past Frank Leboeuf, and this time crossed to Diop. His first shot was straight at the keeper, but luckily, he got a second chance.

Goooooooooooooooooooooaaaaaaaaaaaaaaaaalllllllllllll lllllllllllllll!!!!!!!!!!!!!!!!!!!!!

Super Senegal were beating France 1–0! In Bambali, Sadio and his friends celebrated as if they were the players out there on the pitch in Seoul. They threw their shirts down on the dusty ground and danced around them joyfully.

The next sixty minutes were hard for the Senegal fans to watch, but somehow, they held on for a famous victory. Sadio was bursting with pride for his home nation. What a start for The Lions of Teranga in World Cup football! After draws against Denmark and Uruguay, they were through to the second round.

Next up: Sweden. They took an early lead, but Senegal fought back brilliantly. Henri Camara equalised in the first-half, and then in extra-time, he scored the golden goal.

'Tomorrow, I'm going to play as Camara instead!' Sadio announced passionately.

Sadly, Senegal's wondrous World Cup ended in the quarter-finals against Turkey, but the team's amazing achievements lived on, especially in the minds of their future football stars. Sadio had already known what he wanted to do, but now, he was more determined and inspired than ever. He couldn't wait to follow in the footsteps of Diouf and co, and make national football history of his own.

CHAPTER 4

"RONALDINHO"

Sadio had a special football talent, but what could he do to get himself noticed? Senegal's top scouts didn't bother visiting villages like Bambali. The journey down from Dakar – the home of Diouf, Diop, Fadiga *and* Camara – was too long and too difficult: 400 kilometres of uneven roads, plus a ferry across the River Gambia. If he wanted them to see him play, Sadio would have to travel up to the capital city himself.

'I'll go there as soon as I finish high school,' he told himself in secret.

Until then, Sadio would just have to be the star of the Sédhiou region. He saved his best displays for the village tournaments.

'Bambali can beat anyone,' his friend Boubacar

declared confidently. 'You know why? Because we've got "Ronaldinho"!'

That's what the local people were calling Sadio now. With the ball at his feet, he could dance his way through defences so easily, just like the Brazilian did for Barcelona.

Sadio didn't mind that nickname at all. It was a huge honour to be compared to such a legend. Along with Diouf, 'Ronaldinho' was his favourite football hero. Sadio loved the way that he always looked to attack and entertain.

That was Sadio's style too. He wanted to win *and* have fun on the football pitch at the same time. And in Sédhiou, there was no one who could stop him. If he didn't score Bambali's goal himself, Sadio usually set it up for Boubacar.

'Thanks, "Ronaldinho"!'

Word soon spread about Sadio's skills. People came from nearby villages and cities just to watch Bambali's boy wonder play, and he didn't disappoint them. Sadio loved to perform in front of an audience.

As soon as he got the ball on the left wing,

ZOOM! he used his sudden burst of speed to sprint past the opposition right-back.

'That boy's faster than lightning!'

Sadio dribbled towards the box, until he came face-to-face with TWO big, strong centre-backs.

'YOU'RE NOT GETTING PAST US!' they boomed.

That didn't scare Sadio, though. With a football at his feet, he was fearless. He just needed a plan...

As he dribbled forward, he did one stepover, then another, then another. Which way would he go? The big centre-backs tried their best to watch the ball and not Sadio's flashing feet, but it was no use.

To the right, then to the left! With two quick taps of his right foot, Sadio danced through their clumsy tackles and then fired a shot past the helpless keeper.

Goooooooooooooooaaaaaaaaalllllllllllllllllllll!!!!!!!!!!!!

'Wow, that kid is incredible!'

'He's better than that; that boy is the best footballer that Sédhiou has ever seen!'

Every local club wanted to sign Sadio, but especially the Jules Counda Academy. With Bambali's boy wonder in attack, they could become the best team in all of South Senegal! There was just one problem; Sadio's parents didn't want him to join a football academy.

'I'm sorry, son, but it's time for you to focus on your future,' they told him. 'You must study hard to get a good job when you're older. You won't make money by playing football!'

Sadio was disappointed, but he didn't give up. No, he was determined to prove his parents wrong. When he became a famous footballer, he would earn lots and lots of money. So much money that he would be the richest man in Bambali!

But if he was going to become a famous footballer, Sadio needed to keep testing himself against the top players in Sédhiou.

'I'll come and play for Jules Counda,' he told their coach, Moustapha Kambaye, 'but just don't tell my mum and dad, okay?'

So every week, Sadio set off on his secret football adventure. Sometimes, Moustapha drove him in his car, but sometimes, he had to run all the way to the academy and back.

Thanks to those proper training sessions on a proper pitch, Sadio got better and better. He was learning so much more about football – the tactics, the positions, the best ways to win.

'I thought I already knew everything there was to know about football,' he told Boubacar, 'but it turns out I didn't!'

Sadio would always be grateful to Moustapha and the Jules Counda Academy, but he had his heart set on bigger things.

'One day, I'm going to play in France' – that's what Sadio had been telling his friends for years. They didn't believe him, but he believed in himself, and that was the most important thing.

In order to make that wish come true, however, Sadio knew that he couldn't stand still. No, he had a long road ahead of him and soon, he would need to make that massive next step. It was the only option. He was too good to stay in Sédhiou, so he would have to head to Dakar. Yes, Senegal's capital city was calling him, but would his family allow him to go off and chase his football dream?

CHAPTER 5

LIVERPOOL, 2005

Growing up, Sadio's favourite football teams were Marseille and Barcelona, but he always watched the Champions League final, no matter who was playing. He had to; it was the biggest game of the year!

In 2005, the final was Liverpool versus AC Milan in Istanbul. Sadio crowded around the TV in Bambali with his friend, Youssouph.

'We're definitely going to win this!' Youssouph declared confidently before kick-off.

'We' was Liverpool. That's because after Super Senegal's wonderful World Cup 2002, the club had signed their star player, El Hadji Diouf. Sadly, Diouf had been unsuccessful at Liverpool, but Youssouph still supported them anyway.

'I think it will be 2–1… no maybe 3–1 to the Reds!'

Sadio wasn't so sure about his friend's prediction.
Milan had an amazing team, with world-class
footballers in every position: Cafu and Paolo Maldini
in defence; Clarence Seedorf and Kaká in midfield;
and Andriy Shevchenko and Hernán Crespo in
attack. If they played well, they could destroy a team
like Liverpool.

And in the first half, that's exactly what happened.

Maldini volleyed home Andrea Pirlo's free kick.
1–0!

Shevchenko crossed to Crespo. *2–0!*

Kaká played the perfect pass to send Crespo
through. *3–0!*

The frown got deeper and deeper on Youssouph's
face until at half-time, he'd had enough. 'I can't
watch any more of this – I'm going home!'

'No, stay,' Sadio tried to persuade him, 'you never
know what might happen!'

But it was no use. Youssouph walked off in a sulk
and so Sadio had to watch the sensational second
half all on his own.

First, Steven Gerrard scored a powerful, leaping header. *3–1!*

Then, Vladimír Šmicer went for a dipping long-range shot and the ball squirmed under Dida's arms and into the bottom corner. *3–2!*

Woah, Liverpool couldn't… could they? Sadio couldn't believe what he was seeing. Should he go and tell Youssouph the good news? No, because then he might miss more goals!

Sadio stayed. That turned out to be the right decision because three minutes later, Gerrard burst into the box and just as he was about to shoot, Gennaro Gattuso fouled him.

'Penalty!' Sadio screamed at the TV. It was like the referee could hear him because he pointed to the spot straight away.

It was Xabi Alonso who stepped up to take it for Liverpool. What a massive moment! Sadio felt really nervous and he was only watching; imagine what it would feel like to actually *play* in a Champions League final? The boy from Bambali dared to dream.

'One day!' Sadio told himself excitedly. 'One day!'

Dida dived down low to save Alonso's penalty, but the Spaniard slid in to score the rebound. *3–3!*

'This is crazy!' Sadio said to himself with a smile. It was the most dramatic football match he had ever seen, and he didn't want it to end.

After thirty more minutes of tense extra time, the 2005 Champions League final went all the way to penalties. By then, Sadio was definitely supporting Liverpool. Could they win the shoot-out and pull off the greatest comeback in football history?

Dietmar Hamann went first for Liverpool and... scored! So did Djibril Cissé and Vladimír Šmicer.

Jon Dahl Tomasson and Kaká both scored for AC Milan, but Serginho sent his shot high over the crossbar and then the Liverpool keeper Jerzy Dudek made a super save to stop Pirlo's strike. *3–2 to Liverpool!*

This was it: the crucial spot-kick. It was so nerve-wracking that Sadio could hardly watch. Shevchenko had to score, otherwise it was all over for AC Milan. He ran up and tried to chip it over the diving keeper, but Dudek reached up his right glove and saved it.

Liverpool were the new Champions of Europe!

'Hurraaaaay!'

While the players celebrated on the TV screen, Sadio jumped for joy in Bambali. What a thrilling final! Would Youssouph be happy that Liverpool had won, or furious that he had missed the rest of the match? A bit of both, probably, but Sadio couldn't wait to tell his friend all about it!

It was a night that he would never ever forget. That crazy Champions League final just made Sadio even more certain about his life ambition: to become a famous footballer. Plus, it gave him a new favourite team to support.

Liverpool! Liverpool! Liverpool!

CHAPTER 6

DAKAR CALLING

'Please Mum, please Dad!' Sadio begged. He had kept his promise and finished high school in Bambali. Now it was time for him to test his football talent in Dakar.

'How will I know if I'm good enough, unless I try?'

For years, Sadio's parents had hoped that their son would give up on following his great football dream. They had hoped that he would focus on his education instead. That was how he would get a good job, not by wasting his time kicking a ball around a field.

But it was no use; Sadio wouldn't listen. He was fifteen now and playing football was still the only thing he thought about, and the only thing that he wanted to do. Nothing could change his mind now.

'If this is what you really want,' his parents accepted eventually, 'then we won't stand in your way.'

'Thanks Mum, thanks Dad!' Sadio said, hugging them happily. 'I'm going to make you proud, I promise!'

So, Sadio said goodbye to his parents, and together with his uncle Sana, he started his long journey north to Senegal's capital city to follow his football dream.

Wow, Dakar was like a totally different world from Bambali! Sadio had never seen such busy streets. There were cars, motorbikes and people everywhere, making so much noise. For the first time, doubts crept into his head.

'Am I making a big mistake?' Sadio wondered. 'Maybe my parents were right all along...'

No, he had to stay strong and keep believing in himself. He was here to become a famous footballer. All he needed was a chance to show what he could do.

'Good luck!' Sana said as he set off back to Sédhiou.

When Sadio arrived at the Académie Génération Foot trials, his heart sank. There were hundreds of other boys there, all with the same dream. And unlike him, they already looked like real footballers. They wore Barcelona, Liverpool and Real Madrid shirts on their chests, and cool, colourful boots on their feet. How was Sadio supposed to compete with them?

'All I can do is try!' he told himself and took a long, deep breath.

One of the scouts, Abdou Diatta, walked around, organising the boys into teams. When he came to Sadio, he frowned and asked, 'Are you here for the football trials?'

'Well, duh! Why else would I be here?' Sadio wanted to reply but instead, he just nodded.

'Are you really going to play in *those*?' Diatta asked, pointing down at Sadio's old, battered boots. They looked like they might fall apart at any moment.

Again, he nodded.

'Right, and where's your kit? Don't you have any proper football shorts?'

Sadio shook his head. 'These are the only clothes I have. It doesn't matter what I wear; I'm a future superstar. Just give me a chance to play – you'll see!'

Diatta shrugged and added Sadio's name to his list. It wasn't the first time that he had heard a big boast like that. Most of the time, it turned out to be an arrogant lie, but it was always worth finding out for certain. When Sadio's team took to the field, the scout was watching extra carefully. Was this small, skinny kid really as good as he said he was?

In the first few minutes, Sadio hardly touched the ball. It was a trial and so everyone was trying to show off.

'Hey, pass it!' Sadio cried out on the left wing. 'I've got lots of space over here!'

When, at last, the ball arrived, Sadio suddenly came to life. With his quick feet flashing, he only had one thing on his mind: ATTACK! He danced past the first tackle and then spun his way past the second. He was away, sprinting towards goal at tremendous speed.

The Génération Foot scout wasn't the only one

watching him now. All eyes were on Sadio, just like when he used to be the Ronaldinho of Sédhiou. What tricks would he try next?

That wasn't Diatta's first thought, though. No – he was thinking:

'Okay, so the kid has definitely got silky skills, but does he know when to use them?'

So many kids just wanted to dribble past everyone with their heads down, thinking only of themselves, and not their team. Génération Foot didn't want selfish footballers like that. Was Sadio one of those players?

He was up to the edge of the penalty area now. He had one last defender to beat and one teammate to his right, calling for the ball. It was 2 vs 1 – decision time! Should he play the pass, or go for glory himself?

Sadio faked to go left but at the last second, he tapped it across to his teammate instead. *GOAL!*

'Thanks, mate!' the scorer said, giving him a high-five.

This time, Sadio had set up the goal for someone else; the next time, he wasn't so generous. Instead,

he fired a fierce shot into the top corner himself.
GOAL!

On the sidelines, the Génération Foot scout
smiled. The kid had been telling the truth! He really
was a future superstar, and that's exactly what the
football academy was looking for. Even in those
battered old boots, he was still easily the best player
on the pitch.

At the end of the trial match, Diatta rushed over to
speak to Sadio.

'Well done today – that was *some* performance,
kid! How would you like to come and play for
Génération Foot?'

Sadio pretended to think about it for a few seconds
but really, he was beyond excited about that idea.
This was the opportunity that he'd been hoping for,
the reason for his brave move from Bambali to Dakar.
It hadn't been a mistake, after all!

'Yeah, sounds good,' he said at last, trying his best
to sound calm.

'Great, and don't worry, we'll find you some
proper football kit to wear...'

CHAPTER 7

GÉNÉRATION FOOT

When Sadio joined Génération Foot, the academy
was only just getting started. It was run by Mady
Touré, a former professional footballer who had
played in the French league until he was badly
injured and had to retire. At that tough time, Touré
came up with a bold new plan. This was in the late
1990s, just before Super Senegal's success in 2002,
and he thought to himself:

'There are so many talented young footballers
in this country who never get the opportunity to
shine. What if I started a brand new academy to help
inspire our future superstars and prepare them for
playing in Europe?'

What a great idea! Génération Foot was born, and the academy soon formed a partnership with a club in France. It meant that every year, at least two of the best young players in Dakar would get the chance to go for a trial at FC Metz. That was what had happened to Papiss Cissé, and now he was one of the top scorers in Ligue 2!

Sadio was Génération Foot's newest recruit, and he was determined to follow in Cissé's footsteps. He would do whatever it took to achieve his dream of becoming a famous footballer.

'One day, I'm going to make it big!' he told himself again and again.

The coach, Jules Boucher, noticed something special about Sadio straight away, and so did Touré. It wasn't his speed or his skill, although they were both brilliant. No, what was so special about Sadio was his belief, his quiet confidence. He didn't give up, no matter what.

'That kid has got what it takes to reach the top!' the Génération Foot director declared. He was sure of it.

Sometimes, Sadio did have difficult days in Dakar, when he played badly or missed his family back in Bambali. After all, he was still a sixteen-year-old boy, living a long way from his home. But becoming a footballer was all he had ever wanted to do, and he knew it wouldn't be easy. And with Metz in his mind, he always bounced back stronger.

'That's it – excellent work!' was the reaction.

At the academy, Sadio was learning so much about football, even more than he had at Jules Counda. The coaches were top class and they were teaching him everything he would need to become a superstar in Europe. He could feel his football brain getting bigger and bigger. Rather than just flying down the left wing at full speed every time, he was starting to think carefully about the right decisions to make.

Cross, dribble, pass or shoot – what was most likely to help them win?

For the first time ever, Sadio really felt part of a team. He was still quite shy around new people, but after a few weeks, the other players weren't strangers anymore; they were his friends. Boucher was delighted to see Sadio joining in with all the jokes in the dressing room.

'A few months ago, we couldn't get you to speak,' his coach laughed, 'and now we can't keep you quiet!'

Neither could the defenders out on the football pitch. Week after week, Sadio lit up the Stade Déni Biram Ndao with his electric speed and skill. As soon as he had the ball at his feet, the excitement grew around the ground. What trick would he try next? Which way would he twist and turn?

Soon, people were coming from all over Dakar to see Sadio play, just like they had during his days as the Ronaldinho of Bambali. His goals and assists helped push Génération Foot higher and higher up Senegal's national leagues. By 2011, they were playing in the second division.

'Not bad for a bunch of kids!' Boucher liked to tease them but really, he was extremely proud of his young players. If they kept improving, Sadio and co. could be the future of the national football team.

Since the success of 2002, things had gone

downhill for Super Senegal. They had failed to reach another Africa Cup of Nations final and they had missed out on the 2006 World Cup in Germany too. The golden generation of Diouf, Diop, Cissé and Camara was getting old, so who would take their places?

'Me!' Sadio told himself. So far, he was on track to achieve his football dream but first, he would need to prove himself outside of Senegal, outside of Africa altogether. Europe was where he wanted to go, but how would he get there?

Ahead of the 2011–12 season, the Génération Foot coaches met up to select their two most talented players to send for a trial year at Metz.

The first was an energetic midfielder who loved to tackle and pass. His name was Mayoro N'Doye.

The second was a magical forward who loved to dribble and shoot. His name was… Sadio Mané!

CHAPTER 8

MOVING TO METZ

It all happened so fast that Sadio could only share the great news with his family and friends once he had moved to Metz.

'Mum, can you hear me? ... Yes, sorry, that's because I'm in France!'

'Boubacar, do you remember where I always told you I'd go to play football? Well, guess where I'm calling from right now?!'

Sadio had just arrived at a new club in a new country with hardly any clothes or belongings, but none of that mattered. Instead, he was buzzing with pride and excitement. This was what he had been dreaming about since he was three years old: a huge opportunity to become a European star. The pressure was on, however. His trainee contract at Metz would only last for one year, so if he wanted a professional deal, he needed to make a big impact straight away.

'Let's do this!' he told Mayoro.

There was just one issue, and sadly, it was a pretty big one – Sadio had an injury. At first, he didn't tell anyone at Metz about it because he was desperate to succeed, and he didn't want to miss any matches. He played on through the pain, trying his best to impress.

But as soon as Touré came to visit and saw Sadio in training, he knew that something was wrong. It was like he was watching a totally different player. Where was that sudden burst of speed? Where were those twists and turns?

'What's happened?' Touré asked him afterwards. 'Tell me the truth – are you hurt?'

Sadio looked down at the grass below his boots and nodded glumly.

'Right, well, you can't just keep playing; you'll only make things worse. You need to see a physio and sort the problem out!'

But when Sadio did see a doctor, the news was bad – very bad. He was going to need surgery and that meant several boring months of rest and recovery.

'Noooooooooo!' he groaned. It felt like his big European opportunity was slipping through his fingers.

Everyone tried to console him. 'Don't worry, you'll be back out on the pitch in no time,' said Touré, Mayoro and also his new friend and teammate, Kalidou Koulibaly.

Kalidou was a tall, powerful centre-back who was already playing for the Metz first team. His family came from Senegal, but Kalidou was born and raised in France and he had been at the club for years. So, he became like a big brother to Sadio, looking after him and showing him around the city.

'Me at the back and you in attack – we're going to turn this team around, mate!' Kalidou told him confidently.

That was the hope because Metz were slipping down the table. If they didn't start winning soon, they might even get relegated to Ligue 3. With that threat at the front of his mind, Sadio focused on getting back out onto the football pitch as quickly as possible.

'I'm going to save the day!' he kept telling himself. That thought kept him going during those difficult months.

By December, Sadio was finally back on the training field. It felt so good to be playing again after all that watching and waiting. At first, Metz put him with the reserve team, but not for long. Once they saw Sadio's true talent, they bumped him straight up to the senior squad.

'Seriously, that kid is lightning-quick and lethal on the ball!' the reserve coach told Patrick Hesse, the assistant manager of the Metz first-team. 'Just give him a chance – he'll show you what he can do.'

Hesse nodded, but he wasn't getting his hopes up yet. Sadio was only eighteen years old, and at that age, most players were still learning all the time. They showed flashes of brilliance, but you couldn't rely on them, especially not if it came to a relegation fight…

One training session – that was all it took for
Hesse to change his mind. Because it turned out that
Sadio wasn't like most eighteen-year-olds. No, Sadio
was special. He had everything: pace, skill, passion,
beautiful balance, a great first touch, and a good eye
for a pass too.

Now that his injury had healed, Sadio felt like
his old self again. The sudden burst of speed was
back and so were the twists and turns. To the right,
then to the left, then to the right again – his body
movements made the Metz defenders feel dizzy.
They didn't know what to do. They backed away and
backed away until it was too late.

*Goooooooooooooooooooooaaaaaaaaaaaaaaaaalllllllllllll
lllllllllllllll!!!!!!!!!!!!!!!!!!!!!*

Standing on the sidelines, Hesse couldn't believe
his eyes. 'That kid is INCREDIBLE!' he said to
himself. He knew that kind of special talent could
make all the difference for Metz.

Soon, Sadio was called up to the subs bench.
It was a new experience for him, and one that he
didn't enjoy at all. He wanted to be playing, not

watching! He sat there, slumped in his seat, thinking, 'When are they going to bring me on? This is *so* boring!'

At last, Sadio's first big European opportunity arrived. He came on for the last twenty minutes of their home game against SC Bastia. It was still 0–0 and the game was crying out for a hero.

'Perfect!' Sadio thought to himself as he ran on wearing a dark red Metz shirt with the Number 21 on his back.

He ran and ran, desperate to get on the ball and shine. One moment of magic – that was all it would take to win the game. Sadly, however, it was Bastia who scored the late winning goal.

'Noooooooo!' At the final whistle, Sadio sank to the floor in despair. His Ligue 2 debut had ended in disaster.

'Hey, you played well, kid,' the Metz manager Dominique Bijotat said, patting him on the back. 'Don't worry, we've got plenty more matches ahead of us!'

After that, Sadio switched between the starting

line-up and the subs bench. He always worked hard on the left wing, creating chances for the team, but their results just got worse and worse. Metz slipped from ninth place to fifteenth and then down to seventeenth, just one place above the relegation zone.

'Come on, we're better than this!' Sadio wanted to scream out in frustration. Sadly, he was getting used to that losing feeling, and he still hadn't scored a single goal. What a nightmare! His club was in chaos and now they only had three games left to save their season.

'It's now or never!' Bijotat told his players before kick-off against Guingamp. 'We *have* to win this!'

Sadio did finally score his first goal for the club, but it was too little, too late: Metz had been losing 4–0, so there was nothing to celebrate. They were doomed, and nothing could save them, not even with Kalidou at the back and Sadio in attack.

Relegation was the worst feeling that Sadio had ever experienced, and one that he would never forget. He sat there on the pitch long after the last game of the season was over, wishing that the ground would just swallow him up. His big European opportunity had been a painful failure – nineteen games, one goal and one relegation.

Would Sadio now have to return to Senegal, or would someone offer him a second chance?

CHAPTER 9

STARRING FOR SENEGAL

During Sadio's miserable time at Metz, there was at least one shining light: he became an international footballer!

Aliou Cissé, one of Senegal's superstars back in 2002, was now the manager of the national Under-23 team and in April 2012, he called Sadio up to his squad.

'Thank you, it's a huge honour to be selected!' he replied proudly.

Sadio couldn't wait to represent his country. This was his chance to follow in the footsteps of his heroes, Diouf and Diop, and lead the nation to another major tournament. If Senegal could beat

Oman, they would get to play at the 2012 Olympic Games in London.

'This is our most important football match since 2002,' Cissé told his players in the dressing room at the City of Coventry Stadium. 'We have never qualified for the Olympics before. Go out there and make your country proud!'

'Yes!' Sadio cheered with his new teammates. He could feel the adrenaline rushing through his body. What a moment to make his international debut! The manager had put him straight into the starting line-up, so the pressure was really on for him to perform well.

In the very first minute, Senegal won a free kick out on the right wing. Pape Souaré curled the ball into the box and Ibrahima Baldé leapt high to head it home. 1–0 – what a start!

Sadio still didn't know his new teammates that well, but he celebrated with them like they were his oldest friends.

'Yes, Ibrahima!'

'That cross was a beauty, Pape!'

Senegal! Senegal! Senegal!

After that, they didn't just sit back and defend; no, they went on the attack again. Sadio was linking up well with his fellow forwards, Ibrahima and Moussa Konaté. He even had a few shots on goal, but one went wide, and one was saved by the Oman keeper.

'Unlucky, great play!' Cissé clapped and cheered on the sidelines.

With ten minutes to go, Senegal were still only winning 1–0. They needed a second goal to make the victory safe...

As the ball came to Sadio, he already knew what to do next. He didn't even take a touch to control it; he played a perfect, first-time pass into Abdoulaye Sané's path. The sub striker ran onto it and shot past the keeper. 2–0 – Senegal were going to the Olympics!

At the final whistle, the whole Under-23s squad hugged and danced together in front of the fans. Sadio couldn't stop smiling. Another of his football dreams had come true; he had helped make history for his country.

'London, here we come!'

But before that trip of a lifetime, Sadio received more brilliant news – he had been called up to Senegal's senior team for a friendly against Morocco. And he wasn't the only one.

'Me too!' cheered Ibrahima.

'Me too!' cheered Moussa.

The national team manager, Joseph Koto, was looking to the future; he believed in Senegal's new young stars. So for the match in Marrakesh, he started all three of them alongside one of Sadio's heroes – Génération Foot's finest, Papiss Cissé. What a strikeforce! Sadio couldn't wait to play his part.

In the eighth minute, he tested the Morocco keeper with a thirty-yard thunderbolt. It was heading for the top corner until the keeper pushed it past the post.

'Unlucky!' Papiss clapped encouragingly. 'Great effort!'

In the eleventh minute, Sadio dribbled down the left wing with his orange boots flashing. With a sudden burst of speed, he went past the Morocco right-back and into the box. What next? It was decision time and he had to get it right. Should he shoot? No, the angle was too tight. He needed to cross it, but to who? Papiss was there at the back post, but his pass would have to be really precise to reach him. Suddenly, Sadio spotted Moussa making a great run towards the penalty spot. Perfect! He cut the ball cleverly back for Moussa to hit first time. *1–0!*

'What a pass!' he screamed, lifting Sadio high into the air.

Koto took Moussa off at half-time, then Ibrahima off after sixty minutes, but he kept Sadio on until the last ten minutes. On his Senegal senior debut, he had set up the winning goal.

'Well played,' the manager said, patting Sadio on the back. 'Welcome to the team!'

It was no surprise when Koto picked the same strikeforce for Senegal's next match against Liberia. Together, they were lethal.

In the first half, Papiss crossed to Ibrahima. *GOAL!*

And in the second half, Sadio made a late sprint into the Liberia penalty area to poke the ball in.

Goooooooooooooooooooooaaaaaaaaaaaaaaaaallllllllllllll llllllllllllll!!!!!!!!!!!!!!!!!!!!!

Sadio had scored his first international goal! He ran towards the corner flag with both arms raised above his head, pointing up at the fans. He was so proud to be Senegal's new national hero.

'2012 is going to be the new 2002!'

Sadio counted down the days until the start of the Summer Olympics. It was going to be the greatest few weeks of his life. Senegal would be in Group A, along with Great Britain, Uruguay and the United Arab Emirates. And they would get to play at two of the most famous stadiums in the world: Manchester United's Old Trafford and 'The Home of Football', Wembley.

For Sadio, it would be a chance to win a trophy for his country and also a chance to show off his skills on the big stage. People all over the world watched the Olympic Games.

'If I shine, I could be playing in England or Germany next season!' he told himself.

Sadio was playing in a deeper midfield role for Senegal, but that didn't stop him bursting forward. Against Great Britain, he controlled the game with his quick passing and clever movement. All that was missing was a goal. In the first half, he chipped the ball over the keeper, but it landed just wide of the post.

'Nooooooooooo!' he groaned.

With ten minutes to go at Old Trafford, Great Britain were winning 1–0. Time was running out for Senegal, but their star playmaker didn't panic. Sadio had a plan. He dribbled forward down the right wing, waiting for Moussa to make a run. As soon as the striker set off, Sadio split the defence with a beautiful through-ball. Moussa chipped the keeper too and this time, the ball landed in the back of the net. *1–1!*

'What a pass!' their captain Mo Diamé cried out. 'You're a genius!'

With the whole world watching, Sadio and Moussa had saved Senegal from defeat.

Next up: one of the tournament favourites, Uruguay, at Wembley Stadium. Sadio couldn't wait to play there in front of 75,000 fans. As he walked out onto the pitch, he looked up at all the green, yellow and red Senegal flags and soaked up the amazing atmosphere. Yes, he had certainly come a long way since his days on the local pitches of Sédhiou.

Uruguay had brought their two star strikers to London – Luis Suárez and Edinson Cavani – but they were no match for Super Senegal. Moussa scored two headers in the first half and the Lions of Teranga held on, despite playing with ten men for sixty-five minutes.

'Wow, what a team performance!' Sadio cheered as the players clapped and waved to the supporters in the stadium. He could picture the proud people back home in Bambali, crowding around the TV screen just like he had when he was a little boy.

A 1–1 draw with the UAE was enough to send Senegal through to the Olympic quarter-finals. It was a new amazing achievement, ten years on from the successes of 2002. Again, it was Moussa who scored their goal, but Sadio hoped that he was impressing the scouts too. He was working really hard to pull the strings in midfield.

In the quarter-finals, Senegal faced Group B

winners Mexico. The Lions of Teranga took a while to wake up and after sixty minutes, they were 2–0 down. They didn't give up, though. No, they knew they had the spirit to fight back, and the skill too.

Sadio dribbled forward and passed to Pape on the left. He curled a teasing cross into the box and there was Moussa to head it in. *2–1!*

Senegal were back in the game and a few minutes later, Ibrahima equalised from a Pape corner-kick. *2–2* – what a comeback! Could they now go on and win the match? No, sadly in extra time, their tired defenders made two terrible mistakes to hand Mexico a 4–2 win.

Sadio and his teammates had been knocked out of the Olympics, but the players could hold their heads up high. In their first ever appearance in the tournament, Senegal had surprised everyone with their talent and teamwork.

So, what next for Sadio? Had the scouts been watching his classy performances as Senegal's playmaker? Yes, they had.

CHAPTER 10

OFF TO AUSTRIA

After the 2012 Olympics, one thing was certain; Sadio would not be staying at Metz to light up Ligue 3. No, he was moving on to bigger and better things. He just needed to work out where they would be.

England? There was talk of interest from Premier League giants Arsenal, but in the end, that fizzled out.

Germany? The Borussia Dortmund manager, Jürgen Klopp, was definitely interested, but in the end, he decided to sign Marco Reus instead.

Austria? It wasn't the most exciting league in Europe, but the reigning champions Red Bull Salzburg were on the lookout for new attackers.

Their Sporting Director, Gérard Houllier, had spotted Sadio's special talent straight away. With his bursts of speed and his skill on the ball, the nineteen-year-old had so much potential.

'If we coach him well, that kid could be a superstar!' Houllier told the manager, Roger Schmidt.

Metz needed money desperately, so they accepted Salzburg's offer of £3 million. Now, it was up to Sadio – did he want to go? One day, he dreamed of playing for one of the best clubs in Europe but for now, he was still young and still learning. Salzburg seemed like the perfect place for him to improve as a player. So, just as the summer transfer window was about to close, Sadio was off to Austria!

Arriving in Salzburg was a real shock. When he had moved from Senegal to France, at least the language had stayed the same. But now, Sadio was at a new club in a new (much colder) country *and* he was surrounded by strangers speaking German.

'I can't understand a single word they're saying!' he thought to himself, panicking.

But fortunately, Houllier had arranged for Sadio to stay with a French-speaking family.

'It's just to start with,' the Sporting Director told him, 'until you feel more settled here.'

Phew! That made life easier and allowed Sadio to focus on the most important thing: football. He was determined to become Salzburg's star player as quickly as possible.

After two appearances as a sub, Sadio was ready to start his first match for his new club. However, his opponents, SK Sturm Graz, were definitely not ready.

Just before half-time, Sadio got the ball out on the left wing with his back to goal.

'Surely there's no danger here?' the three Sturm Graz defenders thought to themselves.

They thought wrong. Sadio spun quickly and then twisted and turned his way past the first tackle. Next, he fooled the centre-backs by faking to pass. He even pointed to where he wanted his teammate to be! But then, as the defenders moved across to try to intercept, Sadio slipped through the gap they left behind. He was now one on one with the keeper and he fired a shot straight through his legs.

Goooooooooooooooooooaaaaaaaaaaaaaaaalllllllllllll llllllllllllll!!!!!!!!!!!!!!!!!!!!

Sadio was delighted; it was a moment of pure football magic. It was easily one of the best goals he had ever scored, even during his days as the Ronaldinho of Bambali. The Salzburg fans were up on their feet in the Red Bull Arena, applauding their new star.

They wanted more and so did Sadio. Late in the second half, he snuck between the Sturm Graz defenders again and jumped up to head home the winning goal. *3–2!*

What a feeling! Sadio felt like he could keep running all night long. It was his first full match for the club, and he was already a Salzburg hero.

But could he keep it up? That was Sadio's big challenge. Lots of players could have one great game but only the best in the world – Ronaldinho, Lionel Messi, Cristiano Ronaldo – could do it every single week.

'That's the level I'm aiming for,' he told his teammate, Kevin Kampl.

With each game, Sadio just got better and better. He was learning how to make the most of his superpower: that sudden burst of speed. The Salzburg coaches showed him how to use his pace to play one-twos with his teammates, to make late runs into the penalty area, and to react first to every rebound or mistake. Sadio was becoming an even more dangerous weapon. He set up a goal for his strike partner Jonathan Soriano against Mattersburg and scored himself against Wolfsberger. Then, in the Austrian Cup against Kalsdorf, he grabbed a hat-trick!

'You're unstoppable!' Kevin shouted as Sadio raced off to celebrate.

By December, Sadio was up to eleven goals, including his second hat-trick of the season. His first two strikes against Mattersburg were tap-ins but he saved his best until last. When he got the ball, he was over thirty yards from goal, but he was full of confidence. Why not? He fired a fierce shot towards goal, and it flew like an arrow into the top corner.

As he turned away to celebrate, Sadio waved his hands from side to side as if to say, 'Game over.'

The Austrian Bundesliga had a new superstar. At the end of his first season, Sadio had nineteen goals and ten assists, but sadly, zero trophies to show for them. Salzburg had lost in the semi-finals of the cup and finished runners-up behind Austria Wien in the league. That meant they were into the Champions League qualifiers, but second place wasn't good enough for Sadio. He always wanted to be the best.

'Next year,' Sadio declared confidently. 'Next year, we're going to win everything!'

CHAPTER 11

BEATING THE BIG BOYS PART 1

In January 2014, Salzburg played a midseason friendly against the German giants, Bayern Munich. It was a chance for their players to test themselves against one of the top teams in Europe. And for Sadio in particular, it was time to really shine.

After a slow start to the 2013–14 campaign, he was now back to his brilliant best. With fourteen goals and nine assists, Sadio was almost up to his last season's totals already, and there were still five months of football to go!

'Yeah, but Messi scored sixty goals last year,' he chatted with Kevin, 'and Ronaldo scored fifty-five. I've still got a long way to go!'

With a match-winning performance against Bayern Munich, however, Sadio hoped that he could attract the attention of clubs like Barcelona and Real Madrid. He was ready for the big time; he just had to prove it.

The Bayern manager Pep Guardiola picked a very strong side to face Salzburg. Manuel Neuer was in goal, with Jérôme Boateng and David Alaba in defence, Toni Kroos and Thiago Alcântara in midfield, and Thomas Müller and Mario Götze in attack. What an all-star line-up!

But Sadio felt fearless as he walked out of the tunnel and onto the pitch at the Red Bull Arena. He thought back to the 2012 Olympics, when his Super Senegal had shocked Suárez and Cavani's Uruguay. He was ready to do it again.

On the left wing, Sadio was up against the Spaniard, Javi Martínez. He was a very experienced player, but how would he cope with Sadio's superpower: his sudden burst of speed?

The answer was: not very well. Sadio sprinted past Martínez again and again, to the delight of the Salzburg supporters.

Olé! Olé!

But Sadio knew that his tricks would mean nothing unless his team scored. As he dribbled into the Bayern penalty area, Boateng came across and tackled him clumsily.

'Penalty!' Sadio cried out down on the grass.

But the referee shook his head and shouted, 'Play on!'

That should have been a warning for Bayern, but no. As Kevin got the ball in the middle, *ZOOM!* Sadio was off, racing through the gap between Martínez and Dante. Kevin's pass was perfect, and he dribbled into the box and calmly slotted the ball past Neuer.

Gooooooooooooooooooaaaaaaaaaaaaaaaaalllllllllllll llllllllllllll!!!!!!!!!!!!!!!!!!!!

Sadio ran towards the corner flag with his arms out wide and a focused look on his face. The smiles could wait until after Salzburg had won.

'Thanks mate, what an assist!' Sadio said, giving Kevin a big hug.

Somehow, Bayern still hadn't learnt their lesson.

Five minutes later, a long ball was played over the top for Sadio to chase. He sprinted past Martínez again and got to it just before Dante, who stretched out a leg and fouled him. This time, the referee pointed to the spot straight away – *Penalty!*

Wow, Sadio was causing Bayern all kinds of problems. He was destroying their defence every time. As he got back up, there was still no smile on his face. He really meant business today.

Jonathan stepped up and… scored. *2–0 to Salzburg!*

The game was going even better than Sadio had hoped, but it wasn't over yet. If they weren't careful, Bayern could still come back and win. In the last minute of the first half, Kevin won the ball and played it out to Salzburg's danger man on the left wing.

Sadio dribbled at Boateng, slowly at first, but then with a stepover, he unleashed that burst of speed to leave the defender behind. *ZOOM!* Sadio was into the Bayern box and he crossed to the back post, where Robert Žulj was waiting to volley it in. *3–0!*

'Okay, you can stop showing off now,' Kevin teased his amazing teammate. 'Otherwise, Guardiola's going to sign you before the second half starts!'

Bayern didn't buy Sadio at half-time, but they did try to sign him after the game. Salzburg, however, said no because they were desperate to keep their star player for a little longer, at least until the end of the season.

Although Sadio was disappointed, he didn't complain. He was still only twenty-one, so he didn't mind waiting another few months in order to join a big club. Besides, Salzburg were through to the Europa League Round of 32. Sadio was about to play against another one of the most famous football teams in the world: the Dutch titans, Ajax.

For the first leg, Salzburg were away at the Amsterdam Arena. The stadium was sold out, with red-and-white scarves and banners everywhere. Ajax had a long history of developing amazing young players, ever since the days of Johan Cruyff. Although the club had just sold Christian Eriksen and Toby Alderweireld, they still had highly rated stars like Daley Blind, Siem de Jong and Davy Klaassen.

But Sadio felt as fearless as ever. If Salzburg could beat Bayern, then they could beat anyone. Early on, he dribbled at the heart of the Ajax defence and then threaded a pass through to Alan Carvalho. *Foul – penalty!*

Jonathan scored, and a few minutes later, so did Sadio. Kevin picked him out with a perfect pass, and he coolly rounded the keeper to make it 2–0.

Goooooooooooooooooooooaaaaaaaaaaaaaaaallllllllllllll llllllllllllll!!!!!!!!!!!!!!!!!!!!!

'You're the best!' Sadio shouted, pointing at his teammate.

'No, you are!'

Sadio made sure of the victory during the second leg in Salzburg. He burst into the Ajax box and then calmly nutmegged the keeper.

Goooooooooooooooooooooaaaaaaaaaaaaaaaallllllllllllll llllllllllllll!!!!!!!!!!!!!!!!!!!!!

Sadio took off his gloves and cupped a hand to his

ear as if to say, 'Come on fans, I can't hear you!' The supporters replied by chanting his name:

Mané! Mané! Mané!

First Bayern and now Ajax – Sadio was showing the big boys what a big game player he could be. Sadly, Salzburg lost to Basel in the next round, but he was still pleased with his own performances. Hopefully, he had done enough to earn a top move in the summer. But before that, Sadio wanted to win some Austrian trophies.

CHAPTER 12

DOING THE AUSTRIAN DOUBLE

Could Sadio's Salzburg do the Austrian double? With nine games to go, they were a whopping twenty-seven points clear at the top of the league. They had only lost two matches all season, and with one more win against Wiener Neustadt, the title would be theirs already.

There was a real party atmosphere in the Red Bull Arena, before the match even kicked off. The supporters held their red-and-white scarves high above their heads and sang out loudly and proudly for their favourite football club.

'The fans have come here to celebrate today,' Schmidt warned his players. 'Don't let them down!'

Out on the pitch, Jonathan, the Salzburg captain, gathered his teammates together for the pre-game huddle. 'Come on, let's go out there and give them lots of goals to enjoy! Everyone ready?'

'YEAH!' they all shouted back.

Sadio pulled his socks up and walked towards the halfway line. He was ninety minutes away from winning his first-ever professional trophy. Nothing was going to stop him now.

The Salzburg supporters didn't have to wait long for something to cheer about.

Alan fired a shot past the Neustadt keeper. *1–0!*

So did Jonathan, and then Alan scored again. *3–0!*

As each goal went in, the noise in the stadium grew louder and louder. Salzburg were about to be crowned the Champions of Austria again! One of their star players, however, wasn't satisfied yet.

'Hey, what about me?' Sadio said to his strike partners. 'I want to score too!'

'Don't worry,' Jonathan reassured him, 'there's still thirty minutes to go!'

As Florian Klein dribbled down the right wing,

Sadio used his burst of speed to race into the box.

'Cross it!' he called out.

Fortunately, Florian listened, and his pass was perfect. None of the Neustadt defenders could keep up with Sadio, so he had lots of space and time to pick his spot. He chose the bottom right corner.

Goooooooooooooooooooooaaaaaaaaaaaaaaaaalllllllllllll llllllllllllll!!!!!!!!!!!!!!!!!!!!

At last! Now, Sadio could celebrate Salzburg's success properly. It was his thirteenth league goal of the season and he high-fived his teammates happily.

When the referee blew the final whistle, Sadio threw his arms up in the air. It was trophy time! The Salzburg players ran around the pitch, hugging, laughing and throwing big jugs of beer over each other. It was like they were naughty schoolboys again.

'No, no, NO!' Schmidt cried out as they poured one on their manager's head.

Sadio walked around clapping the supporters with a huge smile on his face. What a season he was having, and it wasn't over yet.

Salzburg still had the semi-finals of the ÖFB-Cup (also known as the Austrian Cup) to play against SV Horn. And now that Sadio had one trophy, he wanted to win another one straight away.

Alan played a great through-ball to Sadio and he finished it off beautifully. *2–0!*

Sadio cut inside and hit a rocket of a shot into the top-right corner. *4–0!*

He raced through on goal again and chipped the diving keeper. *6–0!*

Salzburg were into the ÖFB-Cup final thanks to another hat-trick from Sadio. Once he started scoring, it was like he couldn't stop! As he walked off the pitch with the matchball tucked proudly under his arm, he couldn't wait for the final.

When the big day arrived, however, Sadio wasn't able to play. Was he injured? No, he was suspended.

On the last day of the league season, Salzburg were losing 2–0 to Wolfsberger. What a terrible result! As the game went on, Sadio grew more and more frustrated until eventually he lost his temper completely. Before he knew it, the referee was standing in front of him, showing him a red card.

'Nooooooo!' Sadio couldn't believe it. That one silly mistake would now mean that he missed the ÖFB-Cup final. His teammates would have to do the Austrian double without him.

'I'm really sorry that I let you down like that,' Sadio told them in the dressing room afterwards. He was so annoyed at himself. 'It won't happen again, I promise.'

Jonathan shook his head and smiled, 'Don't worry, mate – we all make mistakes. We'll just have to show you that we're not a one-man team!'

Sadio found it really hard to watch them play without him, but he was there at the Wörthersee Stadium to cheer his teammates on. It was the least he could do after his moment of madness.

'Come on, Salzburg!' he cried.

Their opponents, St. Pölten, played well, but in the end, Salzburg were just too strong for them. At the final whistle, Sadio punched the air and joined the others down on the pitch. It was trophy time again!

'Well done, maybe you don't need me after all!' he

joked with Jonathan, who had scored two goals in the 4–2 win.

The Salzburg captain laughed. 'If we'd had you, we would have scored seven today at least!'

Sadio felt mixed emotions as he went up to collect his winner's medal. On the one hand, he wasn't sure that he deserved it. He hadn't even played in the final! But on the other hand, he had scored a hat-trick in the semi-final, and set up a goal in the quarter-final, and scored one in the Round of 16…

'Actually, maybe I do deserve this!' Sadio decided, looking down at the medal around his neck. There was no time to argue anyway. Jonathan already had the cup in his hands, and he was about to lift it high into the sky.

3, 2, 1… Hurray!

Campeones, Campeones, Olé! Olé! Olé!

CHAPTER 13

EXCITING MOVE TO ENGLAND

After doing the Austrian double, one thing was certain: Sadio would not be staying at Salzburg for another season. He just needed to work out where he would go next.

Germany? Dortmund's star striker Robert Lewandowski had just joined their rivals, Bayern Munich. That meant the team needed a new forward to play alongside Pierre-Emerick Aubameyang. Sadio didn't score as many goals as Lewandowski, but with his pace and skill, he was sure that he was a perfect fit for the club. After meeting the Dortmund manager, his mind was made up.

'Klopp is going to turn me into a superstar!' Sadio told his agent excitedly.

In the end, however, Dortmund decided to buy a pure goalscorer instead – Torino's Ciro Immobile. It was a signing that Klopp would soon regret.

Sadio was very disappointed when his move to Germany fell through, but he didn't give up on his European dream. He had plenty of other offers to consider.

Russia? Spartak Moscow had made a mega bid to sign Sadio. The chance to earn massive amounts of money was certainly tempting, but what about his football career? He was twenty-two now and it was time for him to start playing at the top level.

'Will Spartak be in the Champions League next year?' Sadio asked.

His agent shook his head.

'The Europa League?'

His agent shook his head again.

'Okay, where else could I go?'

England? Southampton were looking for a new forward to replace Adam Lallana and Rickie

Lambert, who had both signed for Liverpool. And the Saints manager, Ronald Koeman, knew the perfect man for the job. He had first spotted Sadio's talent when Salzburg beat his old club, Ajax, in the Europa League. Wow, that burst of speed was incredible to watch! Koeman was sure that Sadio had the potential to become a Premier League star. Plus, he could play out on the wing or through the middle as a striker.

'That's the guy we need!' he told the Southampton Vice-Chairman, Les Reed.

Sadio already knew a bit about Southampton because one of his Super Senegal heroes, Henri Camara, had played for the club back in 2005. However, he would need more information before he agreed to follow in Camara's footsteps.

'Will they be in the Champions League next year?' Sadio asked.

His agent shook his head.

'The Europa League?'

His agent shook his head again. 'But they're a very good team with a great manager. They finished eighth last season, and remember, this is your chance to play in the Premier League!'

That had been Sadio's dream since he was a little boy in Bambali. And if he did well at Southampton, maybe one of the top clubs would come calling, just like Liverpool had for Lallana and Lambert…

'Okay, let's meet them!' he told his agent.

When Sadio met Koeman, he was impressed straight away. In his younger days, the Dutchman had been a superstar defender for Ajax and Barcelona. Now, he was a top manager with ambitious plans for Southampton Football Club.

'We're aiming for the Top Six next season,' Koeman explained, 'and you can help us get there!'

'I'm in!' Sadio said, shaking the manager's hand.

By the start of September 2014, the deal was finally done. For a fee of £11 million, Sadio was now a Southampton player.

'Mané has scored lots of goals for Salzburg,' Koeman told the English journalists, 'and hopefully, he will do the same for Saints!'

Sadio put on Southampton's red-and-white-striped

shirt and posed for lots of photos at the St Mary's Stadium. He had been given the Number 10 and he couldn't wait to wear it proudly out on the pitch.

The new Premier League season had already started, so Sadio had to get up to speed quickly. After a few weeks of fitness work, he was ready to make his Southampton debut in the League Cup away at Arsenal.

The Saints fans were really excited to see their new front three playing together for the first time. The speed of Sadio, the skills of Dušan Tadić and the goals of Graziano Pellè – it sounded like the perfect combination, but would they need time to get used to each other?

No! Alexis Sánchez gave Arsenal the lead, but Southampton fought back brilliantly. Sadio was desperate to make an immediate impact. As soon as he got the ball out wide on the left wing, he dribbled towards the penalty area at top speed.

'Go on, Mané!' the Saints supporters cheered.

With a quick swerve of his body, Sadio cut inside for the shot. It fooled Tomáš Rosický, who dived in for the tackle and tripped him up. *Penalty!*

Dušan stepped up and... scored – *1–1!*

What a start for Sadio! In his first twenty minutes as a Southampton player, he had already created a goal for his team.

After seventy-two minutes of left-wing magic, Sadio was taken off to a standing ovation. The fans had a new favourite player.

'Well played!' Koeman said, patting him on the back as he left the pitch.

By then, Southampton were 2–1 up. Sadio was off to a winning start, and four days later, he was making his Premier League debut against QPR. Could he carry on his fine form?

Yes! Early in the second half, Sadio got the ball out on the left wing with his back to goal.

'Surely, there's no danger here?' the QPR defenders thought to themselves.

They thought wrong. With a clever backheel, Sadio played in Ryan Bertrand to score. *1–0!*

'Thanks, you're a genius!' Ryan cheered as they celebrated together by the corner flag.

Sadio was delighted with his start at Southampton. All that was missing now was a first goal. He thought he had got it in their 8–0 thrashing of Sunderland, but it was given as an own goal instead. So, Sadio had to wait one more week for that magic moment.

It finally arrived in late October, in the first half against Stoke City. Graziano's shot bounced back off the post and straight to Sadio. Surely, he couldn't miss it? With the side of his right foot, he swept the ball into the top corner.

Goooooooooooooooooooooaaaaaaaaaaaaaaaalllllllllllll lllllllllllllll!!!!!!!!!!!!!!!!!!!!!

Sadio watched it hit the back of the net and then raced away to celebrate. At last, he was off the mark for Saints! That scoring feeling was definitely worth the wait. As he listened to the roar of the crowd, he wanted to scream, smile, shout and cry, all at the same time. Sadio was a proper Premier League player now.

CHAPTER 14

SOUTHAMPTON'S HAT-TRICK HERO

Now that he was off the mark for Southampton, Sadio hoped that the goals and assists would start to flow like they had at Salzburg. That wasn't what happened, however. Two months later, Sadio was still searching for a second goal.

'Relax, it'll come!' Graziano kept telling him.

It was easy for him to say that; he had scored eight goals already!

Sadio needed to find his shooting boots again quickly, before Koeman dropped him to the bench. He was playing well, but he couldn't keep missing so many chances. Not if he wanted to become a Premier League superstar.

Sadio played a one-two with James Ward-Prowse and raced into the Crystal Palace penalty area. This was surely it; goal number two! This time, as the keeper rushed out to stop him, Sadio kept his cool. There was no need to panic. He dribbled round Julián Speroni and then chipped the ball into the empty net. *1–0!*

Goooooooooooooaaaaaaaaallllllllllllllllllll!!!!!!!!!!!

'Come on!' Sadio roared with joy and relief.

After that, he was on a roll. He twisted and turned past Joel Ward and crossed the ball to Ryan at the back post. *2–0!*

Yes, Sadio's confidence was back, and so was the song that the supporters had made for him:

All we need is SADIO MANÉ!

Two days later, he sprinted past the Chelsea defence and lobbed the keeper. *1–0!*

Then four days later, he somehow curled a shot into the Arsenal net from an impossible angle. *1–0!*

Everyone was in shock, including his Southampton teammates. 'How did you do that?' they asked, but Sadio just shrugged. How could he explain his special football talent?

With a last-minute superstrike against QPR, Sadio pushed Saints up into third place in the Premier League table. Suddenly, they were aiming a lot higher than just the Top Six.

'If we keep this up, we could be playing in the Champions League next season!' Koeman reminded his players.

That was Sadio's next target but sadly, Southampton couldn't keep it up. They slipped down to seventh, finishing two points behind Liverpool. It was, however, good enough for them to qualify for the Europa League for the first time since 2004. The supporters were over the moon:

Now we've got to Europe,
This is what we'll sing,
We are Southampton,
And Koeman is our king!

For Sadio, there was more good news at the end of his first season in England. On 16 May 2015, he became the proud new owner of a Premier League record! He was already known as one of the fastest footballers around and Sadio confirmed it by scoring the fastest-ever hat-trick against Aston Villa.

It was a match that he would never forget, and it all started in the thirteenth minute. When Paulo Gazzaniga took the goal kick, Sadio knew that Graziano would win the header – he always did. As soon as his strike partner flicked the ball on, *ZOOM!* Sadio was off, sprinting towards the penalty area. He was going to get to the ball first; he didn't doubt himself for a second. The keeper saved his first shot, but luckily, he got a second chance.

Goooooooooooooooaaaaaaaaalllllllllllllllllllll!!!!!!!!!!!!

The St Mary's Stadium was rocking to the sound of his song:

All we need is SADIO MANÉ!

He decided to do a little dance in front of the fans to say thank you.

Sadio had shown it at Salzburg and now, he was about to show it at Southampton too. Once he started scoring, he just couldn't stop! While the fans were still singing, he found the net again. Shane Long pounced on a bad backpass and Sadio reacted first to tap the rebound into the open goal. *2–0!*

Sadio fell to his knees and kissed the grass. He had scored two goals in two minutes – could he make it three in three? Yes!

As Shane dribbled down the left wing, the Villa defenders kept a close eye on Graziano in the middle. Somehow, they didn't see Sadio until it was too late. He was all alone on the edge of the box. As the cross came in, he hit the shot first time, thumping the ball into the top corner.

Gooooooooooooooaaaaaaaaalllllllllllllllllllll!!!!!!!!!!!!

All we need is SADIO MANÉ!

As he ran towards the Southampton fans, Sadio spread his arms out wide as if he could fly. In that magical moment, he felt like he really could!

Sadio had moved to the Premier League to prove himself at the top level, and that's exactly what he was doing. With his first Southampton hat-trick, he had taken another giant step towards becoming a world-class superstar.

And 'The Sadio Show' wasn't over yet. He helped set up one goal for Shane and then one for Graziano.

'Thanks mate, you're on fire!' Graziano said, high-fiving Sadio.

The match finished 6–1, which was Southampton's second highest win of the season. Sadio was very proud of his man-of-the-match performance, but it was only after the final whistle that he found out just how special it was.

'Really? The fastest Premier League hat-trick?' Sadio asked, his eyes lighting up.

Yes, it was true: he had scored three goals in the space of two minutes and fifty-six seconds. He had beaten Liverpool striker Robbie Fowler's record by a full ninety seconds!

By the time he checked his phone in the dressing room, Sadio had so many messages from family and friends. And they weren't the only ones saying nice things about him.

'Sadio was incredible today,' Koeman told the journalists. 'He's still young and he's still learning. Next season, watch out because he's going to be even better!'

CHAPTER 15

BEATING THE BIG BOYS PART 2

As soon as Graziano got it, Sadio was on the move, running from right to left. The Chelsea captain, John Terry, was marking him closely but when the ball came towards him, he missed it completely. Uh oh – Sadio was through on goal!

The Southampton fans at Stamford Bridge were up on their feet, screaming, 'Go on, Mané – score!'

Even with Gary Cahill chasing him and Asmir Begović rushing out towards him, Sadio still didn't panic. He pulled his right leg back as if he was going to kick the ball really powerfully into the top corner, but then squeezed it through the keeper's legs instead.

*Goooooooooooooooooooaaaaaaaaaaaaaaaalllllllllllll
llllllllllllll!!!!!!!!!!!!!!!!!!!!*

So it was 2–1 to Southampton! Sadio slid across
the grass on his knees. As he got back up, he
signalled to the supporters: 'Make more noise!' They
replied with an almighty roar:

SOUTHAMPTON! SOUTHAMPTON!

Ten minutes later, Sadio was causing Chelsea
trouble again. He got the ball in his own half and
burst forward at full speed.

Go on, Mané – score!

This time, however, Sadio decided to pass instead.
As César Azpilicueta came in to tackle him, Sadio
played it across to Graziano, who fired a fierce shot
into the bottom corner. *3–1!*

What a sensational counter-attack from Saints!
Graziano's high-five was so hard that it hurt Sadio's
hands.

'When we play like that, we can win against
anyone!' he shouted passionately.

Sadio smiled his widest smile; he loved nothing
more than beating the big boys. First, against Bayern

Munich and Ajax with Salzburg, and now against
the Premier League champions, Chelsea, with
Southampton. Which top team would be next?

Liverpool! Away at Anfield, Saints were 1–0 down
with five minutes to go when they won a free kick.
José Fonte jumped up to win the first header and then
Gastón Ramírez flicked the ball back across goal. Uh
oh – the Liverpool defenders had made a dreadful
mistake. They had switched off and left Southampton's
danger man all alone in so much space.

Goooooooooooooooooooooaaaaaaaaaaaaaaaallllllllllllll
lllllllllllllll!!!!!!!!!!!!!!!!!!!!

The score was 1–1 – Sadio to the rescue!
'Yesssss!' he cried out as his teammates raced over to
congratulate him on another big game goal.

All we need is SADIO MANÉ!

Liverpool should have learnt their lesson then,
but they didn't. Five months later, back at St Mary's,
they stormed into an early 2–0 lead, but then let it
slip again. And who saved the day for Southampton?
Sadio, of course!

When he came on at half-time, he changed the

game completely. He missed a penalty, but that only seemed to spur him on even more. He had to make it up to his teammates. He twisted and turned away from Mamadou Sakho and then lashed a left-foot strike past Simon Mignolet. *2–1!*

'Come on!' Sadio shouted to his teammates as they ran back for the restart.

Thanks to him, Saints were back in the game, and with ten minutes to go, Graziano curled a shot into the top corner. *2–2!*

'Let's go and win this!' their captain José urged them on. 'There's still time!'

Sadio was determined to be Southampton's big game hero. With his speed and skill, he only needed a few seconds. James Ward-Prowse won the ball back and passed to Graziano, who played it through to Sadio.

Go on, Mané – score!

Sakho tried his best to muscle him off the ball, but Sadio was too strong and too quick. From just inside the penalty area, he aimed an accurate shot into Mignolet's bottom corner.

Goooooooooooooooooooooaaaaaaaaaaaaaaaaaallllllllllll llllllllllllll!!!!!!!!!!!!!!!!!!!!!

It was 3–2 – what an incredible comeback! At first, Sadio the super sub played it cool. But when he reached the corner flag and looked up at all the ecstatic faces, he changed his mind. A classic victory deserved a classic celebration. So what if he got a yellow card for it? Off came Sadio's shirt!

'Hurraaaaay!' cheered the fans.

'Hurraaaaay!' cheered his teammates.

Southampton's heroes shared a big group hug, and even their manager joined in. Koeman ran along the touchline, punching the air.

'Yes, lads – you did it!'

Scoring the winner against Liverpool was Sadio's new number one Premier League moment, even better than his record-breaking hat-trick against Aston Villa.

However, by the time the 2015–16 season ended, Sadio had another new favourite highlight. When Manchester City arrived at St Mary's in May, they were determined to pick up all three points. Leicester had already won the league title, but City wanted to finish second ahead of Tottenham and Arsenal.

Southampton, however, had other ideas. They needed a victory too if they wanted to finish seventh and qualify for the Europa League again. Plus, their star man Sadio was stuck on seven Premier League goals, and that was nowhere near good enough. He was desperate to reach double figures, at least.

'This season, we've beaten Chelsea, Arsenal, Manchester United *and* Liverpool,' Sadio reminded his teammates before kick-off. 'Come on, City are the only big boys left to beat!'

Southampton started strongly – Dušan crossed to Shane, who nutmegged Joe Hart. *1–0!*

'That's it!' Sadio shouted as the team celebrated together. 'More!'

A few minutes later, he sprinted through the middle, and Dušan slipped the ball through to him. The pass was so good that Sadio shot first time.

Goooooooooooooooooooooaaaaaaaaaaaaaaaalllllllllllll llllllllllllll!!!!!!!!!!!!!!!!!!!!

Now it was 2–0! By the corner flag, Sadio waved

his arms up and down to give the supporters the signal. They replied with another almighty roar:

SOUTHAMPTON! SOUTHAMPTON!

Early in the second half, Sadio scrambled in his second goal of the game. *3–1!*

Could he be Saints' hat-trick hero again? Yes! As Dušan dribbled forward, Sadio burst through the City defence.

'Now!' he shouted, pointing at the space in front of him.

With his first touch, Sadio entered the penalty area. With his second, he slid the ball under Hart's outstretched arm.

Gooooooooooooooooooooaaaaaaaaaaaaaaaallllllllllll llllllllllllllll!!!!!!!!!!!!!!!!!!!!

The score was 4–1 – Game Over! As the Saints fans cheered, Sadio bounced up and down, holding up three fingers on each hand. Another hat-trick, and against Manchester City too!

'If only we played the big boys every week,' Shane teased him. 'You'd be the top scorer in the Premier League!'

CHAPTER 16

LOVE FROM LIVERPOOL

Now that he had beaten all the Premier League big boys, surely one of them would want to buy him?

As much as Sadio loved playing for Southampton, he had his heart set on reaching the highest level. If he could get twenty-five goals and fourteen assists in two seasons at Saints, imagine what he could do in a team filled with world-class superstars.

'I'm ready for the next step now!' Sadio believed in himself and his plan worked perfectly. In 2016, he had not one but TWO top English teams fighting to sign him.

The Manchester United manager, Louis van Gaal, was looking to add some extra pace to his attack, and he made Sadio his number one priority to be signed.

'How would you like to come and play for one of the biggest clubs in the world?' van Gaal asked. 'You'll be part of an exciting new team that's going to take us back into the Champions League next year.'

Sadio thought long and hard about signing for United, but in the end, he said no. It felt like the wrong move to make, and for the wrong manager too.

After seven successful seasons at Borussia Dortmund, Jürgen Klopp was now in charge of Liverpool. Like van Gaal at United, he was building a brand new team to challenge for Europe's top trophies: the Premier League title and the Champions League. And there was one super-fast forward at the top of Klopp's shopping list.

'I made a massive mistake when I didn't sign you at Dortmund,' he admitted to Sadio, 'but now, we've got a second chance to work together!'

Klopp wasn't taking 'no' for an answer, especially after Sadio's sensational performances for Southampton against Liverpool. He needed to have him in his team at last!

Fortunately, Sadio felt the same way. He had been waiting to work with Klopp for years. The German manager liked his teams to press their opponents high up the pitch and then attack with pace. They were a perfect match; Sadio was sure of it.

And playing for a big club like Liverpool? Well, it was meant to be! Sadio thought back to that night in Bambali when he had watched them come back to beat AC Milan in the 2005 Champions League final. As a thirteen-year-old boy, he had dreamt of wearing the famous red shirt and now, it was about to become a reality.

'No way!' Youssouph shouted down the phone in disbelief. 'My friend is signing for my favourite team? Man, that's the best news ever!'

There would be no Champions League football to start with, but Sadio was confident that Liverpool would get there soon. Players like Philippe Coutinho and Roberto Firmino belonged at the top level, and so did Sadio.

'Let's do this!' he told his agent eagerly.

At £34 million, Sadio became the new most

expensive African footballer ever. That price tag came with lots of pressure, but he could handle it. He was joining a club that wanted him, with a manager who believed in him. What could be better than that? He was ready to work as hard as he could to help Liverpool succeed.

'Today is a big day and I am very happy to sign for one of the biggest clubs in Europe,' Sadio told the Liverpool website, while happily holding up the famous red shirt with '19 MANÉ' on the back.

For the Southampton fans, it was the same old story.

'Great, we've lost our best player to Liverpool yet again!' they groaned. 'Why? They're not even that good anymore; we finished three points ahead of them last season!'

Sadio felt sorry for his old club, but he was sure that he was making the right decision. With Klopp in charge, Liverpool would soon be rising up the Premier League table.

Their first match of the 2016–17 season was a tough trip to Arsenal. Sadio would be making his

Liverpool debut at the Emirates, the same stadium where he had made his Southampton debut two years earlier. That day, he had won a penalty for his team – so, how would he get on this time?

With one minute left in the first half, Liverpool were losing 1–0. Sadio passed to Philippe and kept running for the one-two. Philippe, however, was fouled before he could pass it back. *Free kick!* The little Brazilian stepped up and curled it into the top corner. *1-1!*

'Come on!' their captain Jordan Henderson cried out.

That was exactly what Liverpool needed, and early in the second half, they took control of the game.

Gini Wijnaldum set up Adam Lallana. *2–1!*

Nathaniel Clyne crossed to Philippe. *3–1!*

Sadio celebrated each goal with his new teammates, but he wasn't satisfied. He was desperate to make a big impact on his Liverpool debut, but so far, nothing! No goals, no assists. Sadio looked up at the stadium screen: sixty minutes gone. Time was running out.

'Klopp's going to take me off if I don't do something special soon,' he worried.

When Adam played it down the right wing, Sadio burst between the Arsenal defenders to get to the ball first. As he sped past Calum Chambers, the defender tried to pull him back, but Sadio shrugged him off. Nothing could stop him now. He cut inside past Nacho Monreal and into the penalty area…

'Pass!' Roberto and Philippe cried out in the middle, but Sadio decided to go for goal instead. It was his Liverpool debut, after all. With his left foot, he fired the ball into the top corner.

Gooooooooooooooooooooaaaaaaaaaaaaaaaalllllllllllll llllllllllllll!!!!!!!!!!!!!!!!!!

It was 4–1! Sadio was off the mark at Liverpool, and with an absolute wonderstrike! He weaved his way through his delighted teammates and over to the touchline, pointing at his new manager. When he reached Klopp, he jumped up on his back and punched the air with glee.

'That goal was for you, boss. You're the best!'

CHAPTER 17

MERSEYSIDE MATCHWINNER

19 December 2016, Goodison Park

Sadio had experienced local football rivalries before
– Salzburg vs Wacker Innsbruck, Southampton
vs Bournemouth. Those matches were nothing,
however, compared to the Merseyside Derby:
Liverpool vs Everton.

'I hope you're ready for this!' Jordan turned and
said to Sadio as the two teams waited in the tunnel
at Goodison Park. The atmosphere was already
electric, and the players weren't even out on the
pitch yet.

Sadio nodded confidently; he had been ready
for months! He couldn't wait to star in his first

Merseyside derby. Liverpool were third in the
Premier League table and with a win over their local
rivals, they could even leapfrog Manchester City into
second place. As long as they finished in the top four
at the end of the season, Sadio would finally achieve
his dream of playing in the Champions League.

But Liverpool needed to bounce back quickly after
losing to Bournemouth and drawing with West Ham.
That meant that the Merseyside derby was now a
must-win match for them. Sadio was off to a strong
start at his new club – seven goals and seven assists –
but with one moment of magic at Goodison Park, he
knew that he could become a real fans' favourite.

'They'll remember me forever if I score,' Sadio told
himself, clenching his fists with determination.

When it was finally time for the teams to walk out
onto the pitch, the noise sent shivers of excitement
down his spine. Wow – it sounded like millions of
people were singing, not just 40,000! Most of the
stadium was bathed in Everton blue, but there was a
loud, proud corner of Liverpool red.

With Philippe out injured, there was even

more pressure on Sadio and Roberto to perform. Fortunately, they had developed a great understanding already. It was as if they'd been playing together for years.

'One of us is going to score today, okay?' Roberto said, flashing his bright-white smile.

Again, Sadio nodded confidently. But for the first thirty minutes, he struggled to get into the game. Everton were defending well, and Liverpool's few shooting chances fell to Gini instead.

'Keep going!' Klopp clapped and cheered on the sidelines.

Sadio jumped up and dummied James Milner's pass. The ball ran through to Gini, who played it out wide to Nathaniel Clyne, who crossed to Divock Origi… but his shot flew high over the crossbar.

'Ohhhhhhhh!' groaned the Liverpool fans.

'Booooooooooo!' jeered the Everton fans.

Early in the second half, Roberto raced onto James's long ball. He showed his strength to hold off the Everton centre-back, but he couldn't beat their keeper, Maarten Stekelenburg.

Ohhhhhhhh!

When the rebound fell to Roberto, he chipped the ball back into the box. Sadio was there waiting, but the cross was behind him. So, he backed away and then leapt up for an acrobatic overhead kick... but he missed and collided with his teammate Adam instead.

Ohhhhhhhh!

Were Liverpool ever going to score? They created chance after chance:

Sadio played a one-two with Roberto, but Leighton Baines intercepted the return pass just in time.

Next, Sadio crossed to Divock, but Séamus Coleman slid in at the last second.

'Keep going!' Klopp urged his players once more. He never stopped believing in his Liverpool team.

For the last ten minutes of the match, they attacked the Everton penalty area again and again. Sadio wasn't giving up until the final whistle blew. He stayed alert, hoping for one last chance to be Liverpool's derby day hero. In a big game like this, they needed a big game player to step forward...

In injury time, their sub striker Daniel Sturridge dribbled across the field, from right to left. Sadio called for the pass, but Daniel decided to shoot instead. Although it wasn't the most powerful kick, it was very accurate. The ball rolled slowly past the diving Everton keeper, towards the bottom corner… but bounced back off the post.

Ohhhhhhhh!

So close! It wasn't over yet, though. There were two defenders in front of him, but Sadio reacted first. With a sudden burst of speed, he won the race and blasted the ball into the empty Everton net.

Gooooooooooooooooooooaaaaaaaaaaaaaaaalllllllllllll llllllllllllllll!!!!!!!!!!!!!!!!!!!!

Sadio was the Merseyside matchwinner! It was an amazing moment that he would remember for the rest of his life. He felt ten feet tall as he raced over to the loud Liverpool corner, waving his arms up and down. He wanted them to make *even* more noise.

'You hero!' Roberto screamed, jumping up on Sadio's back. Soon, the players were surrounded by a cloud of thick smoke, but that didn't stop their celebrations. A last-minute win against their local rivals; what a perfect present for all the Liverpool fans, just a week before Christmas. Thanks to Sadio, the city was RED!

As soon as the game was over, Klopp ran over to Liverpool's hero and gave him a great big hug. 'Congratulations, Sadio – I knew that we could rely on you to save the derby day!'

CHAPTER 18

2017 AFRICA CUP OF NATIONS

A few weeks after his Merseyside derby magic, Sadio waved goodbye to England. He was off to Gabon to lead Senegal to glory in the 2017 Africa Cup of Nations.

'Good luck!' his Liverpool teammates told him but secretly, they hoped that his team didn't do very well. That's because they wanted Sadio back at Anfield as soon as possible. They needed him!

But so did Senegal. Although Sadio had played at the 2015 tournament in Equatorial Guinea, he had arrived late due to an injury. And by the time he got there, it was already too late. His team was knocked out in the group stage, without winning a single game. How humiliating!

Two years later, Sadio was determined to do much better. In fact, his aim was to follow in the footsteps of the Super Senegal of 2002 and make it all the way to the final. Why not? The former Under-23s coach, Aliou Cissé, was now the manager of the senior team and the Lions of Teranga looked stronger than ever.

Their rock at the back was Sadio's old Metz teammate, Kalidou Koulibaly, who now played for Napoli. No one was getting past him!

In central midfield, Senegal had two more Premier League players. Their captain, Cheikhou Kouyaté, played for West Ham, while Idrissa Gueye played for Liverpool's rivals, Everton.

'Don't worry, I won't mention the derby, I promise!' Sadio joked as they travelled together.

In attack, there was Stoke City's Mame Diouf, Génération Foot's next big thing, Ismaïla Sarr, and, of course, Sadio! He was Senegal's number one superstar, and thanks to him, they were one of the favourites to win the whole tournament. Could they live up to the great expectations?

It all started well. In the eighth minute against Tunisia, Cheikhou passed to Sadio just inside Senegal's own half. He had his back to goal, but Sadio spun brilliantly and then *ZOOM!* – he was away, past one player, then another and another. On the edge of the penalty area, he poked a pass through to Cheikhou, who was fouled as he tried to cross it. *Penalty!*

'Great ball!' Cheikhou shouted, giving his teammate a high-five. 'Now, score!'

Sadio placed the ball down on the spot and then waited for the referee's whistle. When it sounded, he took a few steps forward and sent the keeper the wrong way.

Goooooooooooooooooooooaaaaaaaaaaaaaaaaalllllllllllllll llllllllllllll!!!!!!!!!!!!!!!!!!!!!

At last, Sadio had his first Africa Cup of Nations goal. Despite everything that he had already achieved, it was still one of his proudest moments in football. Making his country proud meant so much to him. He raced along the touchline, waving his

green-and-yellow shirt at the supporters above. The
substitutes jumped off the bench to celebrate with
him too.

Senegal! Senegal! Senegal!

In the second match against Zimbabwe, Sadio
was on the scoresheet again. This time, Idrissa won
the ball in midfield and played it to Keita Baldé on
the left wing. His shot was rolling wide, but luckily,
Sadio sprinted in at the back post.

*Goooooooooooooooooooaaaaaaaaaaaaaaaaaalllllllllllll
lllllllllllllll!!!!!!!!!!!!!!!!!!!*

'Come on, this is our year!' Cheikhou cheered,
hugging Sadio and Idrissa tightly.

But Sadio wasn't getting carried away just yet. He
hardly even smiled as he ran back for the restart.
There was still plenty of work to do.

With two wins out of two, Senegal were through
to the Africa Cup of Nations quarter-finals. To
celebrate, Cissé decided to give Sadio a well-deserved
rest for the final group game against Algeria.

'I know you want to play,' his manager explained,
'but we need you fit and firing for the next round.'

Their quarter-final would be a rematch of the 2002 final – Senegal vs Cameroon. That night, the match had finished 0–0 and Senegal had lost in the worst possible way: a penalty shoot-out. So, could Sadio and co. put things right fifteen years later?

'It's time for revenge!' Cissé told his team in the dressing room. Their manager was speaking from experience; he had been the Senegal captain back in 2002, and he had even missed a penalty in the final.

The Lions of Teranga were pumped up as they made their way out onto the pitch in Franceville. However, it would turn out to be a very frustrating night for Senegal. Although they dominated the game, they just couldn't score a goal. First, Cheikhou put the ball over the bar, and then Mame's header was cleared off the line.

'Uh oh, this feels like 2002 all over again!' their supporters groaned in the stands.

As the minutes ticked by, Sadio dropped deeper into a midfield playmaker role. Senegal only needed one moment of magic. The country was counting on him and he couldn't let them down. So, what chances could he create for his teammates?

In extra time, Sadio dribbled in off the right wing, waiting for their sub striker Moussa Sow to make his run. As soon as he set off, Sadio slid the ball into his path. Was this going to be the match-winning moment? The fans were up on their feet, ready to celebrate. Moussa struck his shot powerfully… but the Cameroon keeper saved it.

'Noooooooo!' Sadio cried out with his hands on his head.

Would that be Senegal's last chance to score? No, somehow Sadio managed to split the Cameroon defence once more with another perfect pass. In the middle, Moussa stretched out his long right leg towards the ball… but he couldn't quite reach it.

Game over – time for penalties! It really was the 2002 final all over again, but this time, could Senegal change the ending to the story?

Cissé had his list of takers ready: Kalidou, then Kara Mbodji, then Moussa, then Henri Saivet, and finally, Sadio.

'Maybe they won't need me!' he thought to himself. But if they did need him, Sadio was ready for the responsibility. He would step up for Senegal's fifth and final spot-kick.

Kalidou scored first and then so did the next seven takers. *4–4!*

It was Sadio's turn to make the long walk from the halfway line to the penalty area. He tried his best to ignore the tension in the air and focus on the task ahead – scoring his penalty-kick.

'Relax, this is no different to the one you scored against Tunisia,' he told himself.

Sadio flicked the ball up with his foot and rolled it between his hands, before kissing it and placing it down on the spot. He looked down at the ball and then up at the target.

'You can do this!' Sadio muttered to himself.

He took a few steps forward and then aimed for goal. The Cameroon keeper had dived down to his right, but he managed to stretch up his left arm.

SAVED!

Sadio turned away in disappointment. Why hadn't

he struck the ball harder? Or higher? Or aimed it further into the corner? But it was too late to take it back, and the shoot-out wasn't over yet.

'Please save this!' Sadio begged the Senegal goalkeeper, Abdoulaye Diallo.

'I'll do my best,' he replied.

But sadly, Vincent Aboubakar's penalty was absolutely unstoppable. As the Cameroon players jumped for joy, Sadio sank to his knees with tears streaming down his face. He was so distraught that his manager had to help him off the field.

'I'm so sorry,' Sadio sobbed, 'I let everyone down!'

But Cissé shook his head. 'No, you didn't – you did us proud. You're a national hero and you'll have plenty more chances to prove it. Starting with the 2018 World Cup!'

CHAPTER 19

KLOPP'S NEW-LOOK LIVERPOOL

Although Sadio was devastated that his 2017 Africa Cup of Nations was over, the Liverpool fans were delighted. Their Senegalese superstar would be coming home early! Without Sadio, the team had only managed to draw with Manchester United and then lose to Swansea City. Hopefully, he would help them to return to winning ways.

'Welcome back!' Klopp said, putting an arm around his player's shoulder. 'We've really missed you!'

The Liverpool manager had phoned Sadio straight away after his penalty shoot-out pain. 'Look, you don't have to rush straight back to England. Why don't you take some time off to relax and recover?'

'Thanks, but no thanks,' Sadio replied. 'I want to get back out on the football pitch as soon as possible!'

So, three days after Senegal's quarter-final defeat, Sadio was on the Liverpool subs bench against Chelsea. He couldn't help them win that game, but he did score two goals in two minutes against Tottenham.

The first was a classic Sadio strike. When Gini got the ball in midfield, Sadio was off, bursting through the Spurs defence at top speed. The pass was perfect, leaving him with just the keeper to beat. As he went to shoot, Sadio slipped, but he still managed to scoop the ball into the top corner.

Goooooooooooooooooooooaaaaaaaaaaaaaaaaaallllllllllll llllllllllllll!!!!!!!!!!!!!!!!!!!!

Often, Sadio celebrated his goals like they were no big deal, but not that one. He threw his arms up triumphantly and then leapt high into the air. At last, he was putting his Senegal disappointment behind him.

'It's great to have you back!' James shouted above the Anfield roar.

It was great to *be* back. Sadio's second goal was
a lot simpler. In a flash, he stole the ball off Eric
Dier, dribbled into the penalty area and crossed it to
Adam. His shot was saved, and so was Roberto's, but
Sadio smashed it in at the third attempt. *2–0!*

That was his eleventh Premier League goal of the
season, matching his best ever total at Southampton.
Sadio was also now Liverpool's top scorer, ahead of
Roberto *and* Philippe.

'What would we do without you?' his teammates
cheered.

Unfortunately, Liverpool would have to play the
final eight games of the season without him.

Sadio's second Merseyside derby started so
well, too. He burst past Ashley Williams into the
Everton box and then fired a shot through Matthew
Pennington's legs and into the bottom corner.

It was 1–0! Sadio raced over to Klopp and then slid
across the grass.

'Why do you hate Everton so much?' Dejan
Lovren teased his teammate.

In the second half, however, Sadio's derby day

turned from joy to despair. As he went to tackle the left-back Leighton Baines, their legs got tangled.

'Argghhhh!' Sadio screamed out in agony. His left knee was bent all the way back, and the pain was excruciating. He didn't need the physio to tell him that it was a serious injury.

Sadio had to miss the rest of the 2016–17 season, but it wasn't all bad news. Even without their top scorer, Liverpool still finished fourth, one point ahead of Arsenal.

'Champions League, here we come!' he cheered happily on the final day.

Although it had been a first year of highs and lows, Sadio was sure that he had made the right decision by signing for Liverpool. With the help of his manager, his teammates and the fans, he was improving all the time, and taking his talent to the next level.

Despite his injury, Sadio still won the club's Player of the Year award and he was also the only Liverpool player to be picked in the Premier League Team of the Year. Wow, what an honour!

'Next season, we'll all be there,' Sadio told his clubmates. It was time for them to challenge for the title.

During the summer, however, Liverpool only made three new signings. Klopp's plan was all about quality, not quantity. He wanted the right players in the right positions. He bought a new left-back, Andy Robertson from Hull City, a central midfielder Alex Oxlade-Chamberlain from Arsenal and a new attacker, Mohamed Salah from Roma, too.

At first, Sadio was a little worried about losing his place. Liverpool now had a fab four up front – Sadio, Philippe, Roberto *and* Mohamed. They couldn't all play in the same team together, could they?

Philippe was injured for the first few games, so it was Sadio on the left, Roberto in the middle, and Mohamed on the right. Klopp's new-look Liverpool clicked straight away against Watford.

Sadio dummied Alberto Moreno's pass and then chased onto Emre Can's clever flick. He had time to pick his spot – top corner, of course.

*Goooooooooooooooooooooaaaaaaaaaaaaaaaaalllllllllllll
llllllllllllll!!!!!!!!!!!!!!!!!!!!*

What a way to start the new season! Roberto
scored the second from the penalty spot after a foul
on Mohamed.

'Mo, it's your turn now!' Sadio joked.

Roberto chipped the ball over the goalkeeper's
head and Mohamed tapped it in. It was one goal
each for Liverpool's fab new frontline!

Two weeks later, the three of them thrashed
Arsenal together. This time, it was Roberto who
scored first with a glancing header. *1–0!*

Then Sadio got the ball on the left wing, and
with a quick shift of his feet, he cut inside past Rob
Holding. It was still a difficult angle for the shot, but
Sadio was feeling confident. He curled the ball into
the bottom corner. *2–0!*

'Mo, it's your turn now!' Sadio joked again.

Mohamed was so desperate to score that he ran
the full length of the field. *3–0!*

With their front three firing, Liverpool had high
hopes for their trip to Manchester City. It was one of

those must-win matches that Sadio loved most.

'I've already scored one hat-trick against City,' he reminded Roberto, 'and now, it's time for another!'

Even when they went 1–0 down, Klopp's new-look Liverpool kept fighting for the ball. That was their manager's message: 'Never give up!'

In the thirty-sixth minute, Sadio chased after a long ball over the top. He could see the City goalkeeper, Ederson, rushing out towards him, but he was so desperate to score, and he couldn't back out now…

CRASH! The two players collided at full speed and both fell to the floor. Sadio got straight back up, but Ederson couldn't. Although he had aimed for the ball, Sadio had kicked the goalkeeper in the face by accident.

The referee gave a free kick to City and then reached into his pocket for a card. Suddenly, Sadio's heart was pounding in his chest. Which colour would it be – yellow or red?

Red!

'I'm sorry, but that tackle was dangerously high,' the referee explained.

Sadio's shoulders slumped as he walked slowly off the pitch. What a disaster! He had been trying to help his team to win, but now they would have to try and do it without him...

But they couldn't. City ran riot against their tired ten men – *2–0, 3–0, 4–0, 5–0!*

It was a major setback for Klopp's new-look Liverpool, but Sadio switched his focus to his next big challenge: playing in the Champions League.

CHAPTER 20

LOVING THE CHAMPIONS LEAGUE

It took Sadio a few games to get used to the Champions League, but he was a fast learner and soon he was flying. It helped that he had such awesome teammates around him.

In the group stage against Sevilla, Roberto flicked on Philippe's corner to set up Sadio for a diving header. *GOAL!*

'Thanks, Bobby!'

Against Spartak Moscow, James Milner crossed from the left and Sadio scored with an amazing, acrobatic volley. *GOAL!*

'Cheers, Milly!'

In their first season back in the Champions

League, Liverpool finished top of their group. It was a great achievement, but they had bigger ambitions than that.

'We can win the whole competition,' Jordan argued. 'Why not? We did it in 2005!'

They had to take it one step at a time, however. In the next round, they faced FC Porto. For the first leg at the Dragão Stadium, Klopp's team tactics were clear: 'Keep it tight at the back and grab an away goal if you can.'

The players followed their manager's instructions perfectly, except instead of one away goal, they got five!

And Sadio scored three of them. The first two were nothing special but his hat-trick goal was a superstrike. With five minutes to go, the ball came to him just outside the penalty area. He had two teammates to his left and one to his right, but Sadio only had one thing on his mind: SHOOT! *Bang!* He struck it beautifully, and the ball swerved past the Porto keeper before he even dived.

Goooooooooooooooooooooaaaaaaaaaaaaaaaaallllllllllllll llllllllllllll!!!!!!!!!!!!!!!!!!!!

Was that Sadio's new favourite goal for Liverpool? He wasn't sure; he was scoring so many!

'Man, I love the Champions League!' Sadio declared at the final whistle, with the matchball tucked safely under his arm.

It had finished 5–0 to Liverpool, and who had scored the other two goals? Mohamed and Roberto, of course! The supporters had a new song for their new 'Fab Three':

We've got Salah, do do do do do do!
Mané Mané, do do do do do,
And Bobby Firmino,
And we sold Coutinho!

Sadio had been sad to see Philippe go to Barcelona, but with that money, Liverpool had been able to buy a brilliant new centre-back, Virgil van Dijk. Sadio was especially excited because they had played together at Southampton.

'Trust me, he's unbelievable,' he told Mohamed. 'With Virgil in defence, we'll be better than ever!'

It certainly looked that way. In the quarter-finals,

Liverpool were up against... Manchester City! For Sadio, it would be a chance to make up for his sending-off in the Premier League match earlier in the season.

'No high tackles, this time, okay?' Roberto teased with a flash of his bright-white smile.

Sadio gave his strike partner a friendly shove. 'You just focus on your game, Bobby, and I'll focus on mine!'

Throughout the first leg at Anfield, the atmosphere was unbelievable. The Liverpool supporters never stopped singing; old classics like 'You'll Never Walk Alone', and newer ones too:

We've got Salah, do do do do do do!
Mané Mané, do do do do do...

The move started with Sadio on the edge of his own penalty area. He won the ball and passed to James, who played it down the line to set Mohamed free...

'Go on!' the Liverpool fans screamed, rising to their feet all around the stadium.

...Mohamed slipped it through to Roberto as he raced into the City penalty area. His shot was saved but he managed to poke the rebound across to Mohamed. *1–0!*

Sadio had sprinted forward to join in, but this time, they didn't need him. When the goal went in, the roar was deafening.

Liverpool! Liverpool! Liverpool!

Sadio didn't think that the stadium could get any louder, but he was wrong.

Alex Oxlade-Chamberlain fired a long-range shot into City's top corner. *2–0!*

Then ten minutes later, Mohamed curled a cross towards the back post. As it floated through the air, Sadio made the perfect run between Fernandinho and Kyle Walker, and headed the ball powerfully past Ederson. *3–0!*

Goooooooooooooooooooaaaaaaaaaaaaaaaaalllllllllllll lllllllllllll!!!!!!!!!!!!!!!!!!!

Roberto pointed at Sadio, who pointed at Mohamed. What a superstar strikeforce!

We've got Salah, do do do do do do!
Mané Mané, do do do do do

And Bobby Firmino,
And we sold Coutinho!

Liverpool were through to the Champions League semi-finals, where they would face Mohamed's old club, Roma.

'They might not be as big as Real Madrid, but they're still a top team,' Mohamed warned. 'They just beat Barcelona, after all!'

But at Anfield, Liverpool knew that they could destroy anyone. Even when Sadio wasted two early chances, they kept attacking and creating chances. If he couldn't score, then someone else would…

Mohamed curled the ball into the top corner. *1–0!*

Mohamed raced through and chipped the keeper. *2–0!*

At half-time, it was all looking good for Liverpool, but Sadio wasn't satisfied. So far, he had scored in every round of the Champions League. That was a record that he wanted to continue.

Thank goodness that Sadio had such awesome teammates around him. Mohamed dribbled down the right wing and passed the ball across to him. This time, he couldn't miss – *3–0!*

'You're the best!' Sadio cheered, giving his friend a big hug.

And Liverpool's 'Fab Three' weren't finished yet.

Mohamed set up Roberto. *4–0!*

Roberto headed in from James's corner-kick. *5–0!*

What a performance! Out in Italy a week later, Sadio scored an early goal, just to make sure: Liverpool were through to the 2018 Champions League Final!

'How many tickets will you get? Can I have one please?'

Sadio had so many requests from his friends and family, and he did his best to make everyone happy.

In the days before the big game, a large box arrived in his home village of Bambali. As the local people opened it, they couldn't believe their eyes. Their famous footballer had sent 300 Liverpool shirts for them to wear! Now, they could cheer him on properly.

'We love you, Sadio!'

Liverpool! Liverpool! Liverpool!

CHAPTER 21

CHAMPIONS LEAGUE FINAL 2018

26 May 2018, NSC Olimpiyskiy Stadium, Kiev, Ukraine

Liverpool had done so well to reach the Champions League Final, but their toughest challenge lay ahead.

Real Madrid had superstars in every position: Sergio Ramos in defence, Luka Modrić in midfield, and of course, Cristiano Ronaldo in attack. Plus, 'The Galácticos' had lifted the Champions League trophy two years in a row.

'We have nothing to fear!' Klopp told the Liverpool players in the dressing room in Kiev. 'We deserve to be here, and when we're at our best, we can beat anyone!'

As he sat there listening, Sadio looked around at his awesome teammates: Virgil and Dejan in defence; James, Jordan and Gini in midfield; and of course, Mohamed and Roberto in attack. Their manager was right; Liverpool had superstars in every position too.

'Come on!' the whole squad cheered together.

In the tunnel, Sadio couldn't help smiling to himself. This was the day that he had dreamed of ever since his first kicks of a football, or at least since watching Liverpool's incredible Istanbul comeback, as a boy in Bambali. So many times, people had told him to give up on his dream, but he hadn't, and look at him now. From Senegal to France to Austria to England, Sadio's journey had led him to this: the 2018 Champions League Final. And he was determined to enjoy every moment.

After all the opening acts, the anthems and the handshakes, it was finally time for kick-off.

Liverpool! Liverpool! Liverpool!

The fans had brought the Anfield roar all the way to the Ukraine. They held up their red scarves with hope and excitement. Could their big game player help them to win the biggest game of all?

Sadio almost got his first chance in the very first minute. Roberto spun near the halfway line and played a brilliant through-ball. Sadio was onto it in a flash, but at the last second, Raphaël Varane slid in to clear the danger.

'Ohhhhhhhhhh!' groaned the Liverpool fans.

Their team's strong start lasted until the twenty-fifth minute. As Ramos battled for the ball, he dragged Mohamed to the ground.

'Arghhhhhh!' he screamed in agony, clutching his shoulder.

Mohamed tried to carry on playing, but he couldn't. With tears streaming down his cheeks, he walked off the pitch.

'I'm sorry, mate,' Sadio said, putting an arm around his shoulder. 'We'll do our best to win it without you!'

It was still 0–0 at half-time, but early in the second half, Real Madrid scored one of the strangest goals that Sadio had ever seen.

Real played a long ball over the top and the Liverpool goalkeeper, Loris Karius, came out to make an easy catch. But as he tried to throw it out to Dejan, Karim Benzema stuck out his leg and deflected the ball into the net. *1–0!*

Sadio couldn't believe it, but there was no time to stomp and moan. With Mohamed off the pitch, he had to step up and be Liverpool's star.

A few minutes later, they won a corner and James floated the ball towards Roberto, Dejan and Virgil in the middle. Sadio, meanwhile, was making his move into the six-yard box, ready to react to any flick-ons...

It was Dejan who jumped highest and headed the ball goalwards. The Real Madrid keeper was about to make a simple save, but Sadio stretched out his right leg.

Gooooooooooooooooooooaaaaaaaaaaaaaaaaalllllllllllll llllllllllllll!!!!!!!!!!!!!!!!!!!

Sadio glanced over his shoulder at the linesman. No flag, no offside. 1–1 – Liverpool were back in the game!

'Yesssssss!'

He threw his arms out wide and then leapt into the air. It was Sadio's tenth Champions League goal of the season, and he had now scored in every single round. There had been more impressive strikes, but this was by far the most important.

'Focus, lads!' Jordan Henderson, the Liverpool captain shouted. 'Let's win this now!'

There was heartbreak to come, however. Marcelo crossed from the left and Real Madrid's substitute, Gareth Bale, scored a breathtaking bicycle-kick. *2–1!*

As he watched the goal go in, Sadio sighed. Oh well, he would just have to score again. Gini passed the ball to him on the end of the Real Madrid box. He danced past Casemiro's tackle and fired a low, left-foot shot towards the bottom corner.

'Curl, curl!' he muttered, urging the ball into the net.

But sadly, it didn't quite curl enough. Sadio's shot hit the post and bounced away.

So close! Sadio stood there with his hands on his head, looking up at the sky. Was that game over? Not quite, but as Liverpool searched for an

equaliser, disaster struck for the third time. Bale
hit a swerving shot and it slipped straight through
Karius's hands. *3–1!*

Now, it really was game over. At the final whistle,
Sadio crouched down in defeat. He had given
absolutely everything to help Liverpool win, but it
just hadn't been enough. Not quite.

'What if that shot had hit the post and gone in?'
Sadio wondered to himself. 'It could have been so
different!'

Klopp walked around the pitch, comforting his
tearful players. He didn't speak; what could he say?
No words would ease the pain of losing a Champions
League final.

Sadio was devastated, but he wasn't giving up on
his dream. This was just the start. After collecting
his runners-up medal, he trudged past the trophy
with his head down. He would only look at it when
Liverpool won it.

'We'll be back!' Sadio told Mohamed firmly. 'Just
you wait and see!'

CHAPTER 22

2018 WORLD CUP

Sadio's busy season wasn't over yet, however. A few weeks after the Champions League final, he was off to Russia to fulfil another childhood football dream. His Senegal side had qualified for the 2018 World Cup!

'Good luck!' Sadio teased Mohamed, who was off to Russia too, to play for Egypt. 'May the best African country win!'

Their friendly rivalry had started when they were both named on the shortlist for the African Footballer of the Year award. They had flown to Ghana together for the ceremony where the winner was announced...

'Mohamed Salah!'

'Well done, you deserve it,' Sadio congratulated his Liverpool teammate. 'But let's see who wins at the World Cup!'

Senegal were aiming high in Russia. It would be their first appearance at the tournament since 2002, but they wouldn't get a better chance to qualify for the second round again. There weren't any top teams like France in their group this time. Instead, they would face Poland, Japan and Colombia.

'We can beat any of them!' Sadio declared confidently before their first match.

He couldn't wait to compete with world-class players like Robert Lewandowski and James Rodríguez. Sadio was now the Senegal captain and he wore the armband with great pride. As the national anthem played, he stood there with his hand on his heart and the team badge.

Senegal! Senegal! Senegal!

Just like in 2002, they got off to a winning start. Every time Senegal attacked, they looked so dangerous. Sadio wasn't playing on the left like he did for Liverpool; he was in the middle, creating chances for his team.

Ismaïla raced down the wing and passed inside to Sadio, who quickly shifted the ball across to Idrissa. His shot flicked off a Poland defender's boot and flew past the goalkeeper. *1–0!*

'Wait, are you claiming that goal?' Sadio teased Idrissa as they celebrated.

'Of course, my shot was going in, anyway!'

In the second half, Senegal secured the victory. Their striker M'Baye Niang sprinted after a bad backpass, beat the Poland goalkeeper to the ball and then passed it into the empty net. *2–0!*

'Brilliant work, M'Baye!' Sadio shouted happily as he ran over to hug their hero.

Next up: Japan. They had already shocked Colombia and they were looking to shock Senegal too. Their captain wasn't going to let that happen, however. As Youssouf Sabaly shot from the left, Sadio moved into the six-yard box, ready for the rebound. It was his lucky day; the Japan keeper spilled the ball and he was in the right place at the right time. *1–0!*

Goooooooooooooooooooooaaaaaaaaaaaaaaaalllllllllllll llllllllllllll!!!!!!!!!!!!!!!!!!!!

It wasn't one of Sadio's best strikes, but that didn't matter. Senegal were 1–0 up and he had scored his first-ever World Cup goal. After all the hugs and high-fives from his teammates, he knelt down to kiss the ground. He was so grateful to be living his dream.

'Come on, stay focused!' said Sadio, returning to his role as captain.

But Japan fought back, not once but twice. *2–2!*

Although Sadio was pleased to win the man of the match award, he was disappointed with his team's result.

'We should have won that!' he told Kalidou, kicking the air in frustration.

If they wanted to succeed at the World Cup, Senegal couldn't give away two sloppy goals like that. They would all have to improve for their final group game, including their captain.

'Sadio Mané can do better,' his manager told the media, 'and he needs to do better against Colombia.'

He was used to playing under pressure, but this

was a new level of pressure. For his club, Sadio was surrounded by other superstars: Mohamed, Roberto, Gini, Jordan. For his country, however, he was the main man, and so everyone expected him to create magic all the time.

'I'm trying!' Sadio wanted to scream.

Winning Group H didn't look so straightforward anymore. Senegal and Japan both had four points, while Colombia had three. With one game to go, anything could happen!

Early in the first half, Keita threaded a lovely pass through to Sadio. As he burst into the box, the Colombia centre-back Davinson Sánchez stuck out a leg. Had he kicked the ball or Sadio's leg?

The referee pointed to the spot straight away. *Penalty!* But when he checked the VAR replays, he changed his mind. What drama!

'Keep going, forget about that!' captain Sadio clapped and cheered.

In the fifty-ninth minute, Poland took the lead against Japan.

Then in the seventy-fourth minute of their game,

Colombia took the lead against Senegal. Sadio could only stand and watch on the edge of the area as Yerry Mina headed the ball home.

'Noooooo!' Sadio groaned, turning away in despair.

If things stayed the same, Colombia would win Group H with six points, and Japan and Senegal would be tied on the same points and the same goal difference. And in their head-to-head match, they had drawn 2–2. So, who would go through in second place? The answer was Japan, because of FIFA's 'Fair Play' rule. They had only picked up four yellow cards, compared to Senegal's six.

'No way!' Sadio wasn't giving up on his World Cup dream just yet. Suddenly, he was all over the pitch, playing every position.

From the right wing, Sadio slipped a pass into M'Baye's path, but his shot was saved by the Colombia keeper.

'Noooooo!'

From the left wing, Sadio chipped a clever cross to Ismaïla at the back post. He was totally unmarked, but he blazed his volley high over the crossbar.

'Noooooo!'

In the middle, Sadio spun and fed the ball through to Moussa Konaté, but at the last second, Sánchez stuck out a leg to stop it.

'Noooooo!'

That was it – Senegal's last chance to score. It was over. They were out of the 2018 World Cup in the worst possible way.

'"Fair Play"?' Sadio muttered moodily. 'There's nothing fair about that!'

He wanted to sit down and cry, like he had at the 2017 Africa Cup of Nations. But he was the captain of his country now, and he had to stay strong. He walked around comforting his teammates, telling them the same thing he had told Mohamed after the Champions League Final:

'We'll be back - just you wait and see!'

CHAPTER 23

TROPHY TIME FOR LIVERPOOL?

Back at Liverpool, Sadio started the new 2018–19 season in style, with two strikes against West Ham.

'Come on!' he roared passionately, pointing to the new number on his back: 10. It was great to be back at Anfield, and an honour to wear the same shirt as club legends like John Barnes, Michael Owen and Philippe.

Another game, another victory: Klopp was turning his team into a mean, winning machine. Their 'Fab Three' weren't scoring quite as many goals as last season, but they didn't have to because their defence was now almost unbeatable. Virgil was Liverpool's rock at the back, and if any striker did manage to get past him, they would then have to get past Alisson Becker, one of the greatest goalkeepers in the world.

'I'm so glad that I only have to face you guys in training!' Sadio joked.

Surely it would soon be trophy time? By the end of January, the Reds had only lost one Premier League match all season. That defeat was to their title rivals, Manchester City, but Liverpool were still five points ahead at the top of the table.

'This is going to be our year!' the fans dared to dream.

And the Premier League title wasn't the only trophy that Liverpool were fighting for; they were also into the Champions League Round of 16 again. This time, they were up against one of Europe's big boys, Bayern Munich. The first leg at Anfield finished 0–0, which meant that Liverpool would need to score away in Germany.

'No problem, we can do this!' Sadio assured his teammates before kick-off.

He had plenty of reasons to feel confident. During his younger days at Salzburg, Sadio had destroyed the Bayern defence, and since then, he had become an even better player. Plus, he was in the best goalscoring form of his life.

With Mohamed and Roberto struggling, Sadio had stepped up to save the day, scoring:

the winner against Crystal Palace,
Liverpool's only goals against Leicester City
and West Ham,
a powerful header against Bournemouth,
a cheeky backheel against Watford,
and then two more against Burnley.

'You're on fire, mate!' Kalidou messaged him.

So, could Sadio be Liverpool's big game hero again versus Bayern?

For the first twenty minutes, the Germans dominated the game, but they couldn't find a way through the strong Liverpool defence. And their 'Fab Three' in attack? Well, they worked hard for the team and waited for their turn…

Deep in his own half, Virgil looked up and spotted

their danger man on the move. *ZOOM!* Even at top speed, Sadio still managed to control the long pass perfectly.

'What a touch!' the Liverpool fans shouted, jumping out of their seats. 'Now, SHOOT!'

But Sadio had work to do first. As the Bayern keeper, Manuel Neuer, rushed out to tackle him, he turned him brilliantly and chipped the ball over the defenders and into the net. *1–0!*

Goooooooooooooooooooooaaaaaaaaaaaaaaaaallllllllllll llllllllllllll!!!!!!!!!!!!!!!!!!

Sadio to the rescue! It was a moment of pure magic from Liverpool's Senegalese superstar. After making sure that his shot had crossed the line, he raced away to celebrate. Even he couldn't quite believe what he had just done! It was the away goal they desperately needed, and yet another Champions League strike to cherish forever.

'Keep going!' Klopp urged his players. 'It's not over yet.'

Bayern did equalise, but in the second half, Liverpool scored two headers to win the game. Virgil got the first, and guess who got the second? Sadio, of course!

Although he was one of the smallest players in the team, he could jump really high and, with help from the coaches, he had worked hard on his technique. So, when Mohamed chipped a cross into the box, Sadio threw himself towards the ball, and his powerful diving header landed in the bottom corner. *3–1!*

There was just no stopping Sadio, or Liverpool. Could they even do the double – the Champions League *and* the Premier League?

After some frustrating draws, Liverpool fell one point behind their English title rivals, but surely City would slip up at some point?

From March onwards, Liverpool won game after game… but so did City. It was the tightest title race in years. As both teams prepared for the final day of the season, there was still only that one single point between them:

Manchester City   95
Liverpool   94

'First, we need to beat Wolves,' Klopp told his players, 'and then we can worry about whether City beat Brighton, okay?'

Liverpool didn't let the pressure get to them. They won 2–0, thanks to two Sadio goals from two Trent Alexander-Arnold crosses.

Job done – now, what about City? Sadly, it was bad news; they had beaten Brighton 4–1. Liverpool had lost the Premier League title race by that one single point.

After scoring twenty-two league goals, Sadio got to share the Golden Boot with Mohamed and Arsenal's Pierre-Emerick Aubameyang. He was also shortlisted for the PFA Player of the Year award and selected for the PFA Team of the Year. Although they were all proud achievements, they weren't the trophies that he really wanted.

'We came *so* close!' Sadio groaned in frustration.

The Liverpool supporters still treated the players like heroes, however. What a season it had been, and their search for a trophy wasn't over yet.

Just five days earlier, Liverpool had pulled off

another incredible Champions League comeback. Move over 2005's 'Miracle of Istanbul' – 2019's 'Miracle of Anfield' was even better! This time, it was against Lionel Messi's Barcelona in the semi-finals. Liverpool lost the away leg 3–0, which meant that they would need to score at least three goals at home.

'No problem, we can do this!' Sadio assured his teammates again before kick-off.

Mohamed and Roberto were both out injured, but with the amazing Anfield crowd roaring them on, anything seemed possible. The Liverpool players were so pumped up for their biggest game of the season so far.

It was Sadio who started the comeback. He pounced on a Barcelona mistake and played a clever pass through to Jordan. His shot was saved, but Divock Origi scored the rebound. *3–1!*

'That's it – keep going!' Klopp urged his team on.

Even as the minutes ticked by without a second goal, the Liverpool players didn't panic. A football match could change in a flash…

Trent's pass didn't quite reach Sadio, but Gini thumped it in instead. *3–2!*

Two minutes later, Gini headed home from Xherdan Shaqiri's cross. *3–3!*

Wow, they had achieved the impossible – Liverpool were level! There were wild celebrations near the corner flag, but Sadio stayed calm. He wanted to win the match before it went to extra time.

With fifteen minutes to go, Liverpool won a corner-kick. Trent was about to walk away and let Xherdan take it, when he suddenly spotted Divock in space in the middle. If he took it really quickly, maybe they could catch Barcelona out… *BANG!* Trent whipped the ball into the box and Divock smashed it into the top corner. *4–3!*

'We never give up, do we?' Sadio screamed proudly with his arms around Gini and Virgil.

Unbelievable – Liverpool were through to their second Champions League final in a row!

So, could they go one step further and win it this time in Madrid? The signs were good. Mohamed and Roberto were both back to full fitness and the team felt relaxed and rested after nearly three weeks without a match!

At last, game day arrived – the 2019 Champions League Final, the end of an amazing season, and Liverpool's last chance to lift a trophy. The only team now standing in their way were Premier League rivals, Tottenham.

They had a strong team with stars like Harry Kane, Son Heung-min and Christian Eriksen, but Sadio was sure that Liverpool could beat them, especially if they got off to a really good start…

Seconds after kick-off, Sadio was already causing chaos in the Tottenham defence. From just inside the box, he tried to play a pass to Jordan, but the ball struck Moussa Sissoko's arm instead. *Penalty!*

'Come on!' Sadio roared with both joy and relief. The 2019 final was already looking a whole lot better than 2018.

Liverpool didn't look back after that. Mohamed scored the spot-kick and then with five minutes to go, Divock made it 2–0.

'We did it,' Sadio cheered at the final whistle.

'WE'RE THE CHAMPIONS OF EUROPE!'

It was the perfect end to his best-ever season: twenty-six goals, five assists, and most exciting of all, one gigantic, glittering Champions League trophy.

That had been Sadio's ultimate aim, ever since his earliest footballing days in Senegal. Back then, it had seemed like an impossible dream for a boy from Bambali, but when had he ever let that stop him? Never! Step by step, and goal after goal, he had worked his way up towards his target. From Dakar to Metz, from Metz to Salzburg, from Salzburg to Southampton, and finally, from Southampton to Liverpool.

What a journey it had been, but it was all worth it. Because Sadio was now a world-class superstar and a European champion.

Turn the page for a sneak preview of
another brilliant football story by
Matt and Tom Oldfield. . .

SALAH

Available now!

CHAPTER 1

EUROPEAN SUPERSTAR

Anfield, 24 April 2018

The atmosphere at Anfield was always amazing
but on big European nights, it was extra special.
The chorus of the Kop started hours before kick-off
and, if Liverpool beat Roma, it would go on for days
afterwards. The fans sang the old favourites like
'You'll Never Walk Alone', and they sang the new
favourites too:

Mo Salah, Mo Salah
Running down the wing,
Salah la la la la la la
Egyptian King!

The eyes of the world were on Liverpool's 'Egyptian King'. Mohamed was in the best form of his life, with forty goals and counting. He had already scored thirty-one in the Premier League and nine in the Champions League. Could he keep shooting his team all the way to the final?

For Mohamed, it was going to be an emotional night, no matter what. First of all, he was playing in his first-ever Champions League semi-final, a moment that he had dreamed about ever since he was an eight-year-old boy. He was following in the footsteps of his heroes like Zinedine Zidane and Francesco Totti.

Mohamed was also playing against his old club. When his big move to Chelsea hadn't worked out, it was Italian football that saved him. At Fiorentina, and then Roma, he had rediscovered his passion, his confidence, and the path to superstardom. He would always be grateful for that.

Mohamed's old manager, Luciano Spalletti, had moved on, but lots of his old teammates were still there – Radja Nainggolan, Stephan El Shaarawy, and his old strike partner, Edin Džeko. In the tunnel, Mohamed hugged each and every one of them.

'Good luck,' he said with a smile, 'may the best team win!'

Liverpool were far from a one-man team. Mohamed was one part of 'The Big Three', the hottest strikeforce in the world. With Sadio Mané on the left, Roberto Firmino in the middle, and Mohamed on the right, the Reds looked unstoppable. Even Philippe Coutinho's move to Barcelona hadn't slowed them down. They had scored five against Porto in the Round of 16 and then five against Manchester City in the quarter-finals too. If the Roma defenders weren't careful, 'The Big Three' would run riot again.

'Come on lads, let's win this!' the Liverpool captain Jordan Henderson shouted as the players took up their positions for kick-off.

Even during his days at Roma, Mohamed had been more of a winger than a striker. With his amazing sprint speed, he would race past defenders and set up chances for Edin. At Liverpool, however, manager

Jürgen Klopp had helped turn Mohamed into a
proper forward and a goalscoring machine. He still
worked hard for his team but he did it higher up the
pitch. That way, if a defender made a mistake, he
was always ready to pounce.

Liverpool created their first good opening after
twenty-seven minutes. One clever flick from Roberto
was all it took to set speedy Sadio away. He had
Mohamed to his right but Sadio wanted the glory for
himself. In the penalty area, he pulled back his left
foot and... blazed it over the crossbar!

The Liverpool fans buried their heads in their
hands – what a missed opportunity! Two minutes
later, another one arrived. Mohamed played a great
pass to Roberto, who squared it to Sadio. He hit it
first time... high and wide!

Groans rang out around Anfield. They couldn't
keep wasting these opportunities! Liverpool needed
more composure in front of goal. What they needed
was a cool head...

Sadio passed to Roberto, who passed to Mohamed
on the right side of the box. With a quick tap of the

boot, he shifted the ball onto his lethal left foot. Time
to shoot? No, not quite yet. Mohamed took one
more touch to get a better angle, and then curled a
fierce strike into the top corner. The technique was
astonishing and he made it look so easy.

*Goooooooooooooooooooaaaaaaaaaaaaaaaalllllllllllll
llllllllllllll!!!!!!!!!!!!!!!!!!!!*

Mohamed put his arms up straight away – he
wasn't going to celebrate a goal against his old team.
That didn't stop the Liverpool fans, though, or his
new teammates.

'Get in!' Jordan screamed, punching the air.

In the last minute of the first half, Mohamed
passed to Roberto near the halfway line and sprinted
forward for the one-two. The Roma defenders had
no chance of catching him. Instead, their goalkeeper
rushed out to the edge of his area to block the shot
but Mohamed lifted the ball delicately over him. So
calm and so classy! As it rolled into the back of the
net, he lifted his arms up again.

*Goooooooooooooooooooaaaaaaaaaaaaaaaalllllllllllll
llllllllllllll!!!!!!!!!!!!!!!!!!!!*

There was just no stopping Mohamed. In the second half, he beat Roma's offside trap again and crossed to Sadio for a simple tap-in. *3–0!*

They pointed over at Roberto. 'Bobby, it's your turn to score now!'

Mohamed picked the ball up on the right wing and attacked the poor Roma left-back, who backed away in fear. Hadn't Mohamed done enough damage for one day? No! He danced his way through and crossed to Roberto at the back post. *4–0!*

Liverpool's 'Big Three' were all on the scoresheet yet again. It was party time at Anfield:

We've got Salah, do do do do do do!

Mané Mané, do do do do do,

And Bobby Firmino,

And we sold Coutinho!

After seventy-five brilliant minutes, Klopp gave his superstar a well-deserved rest. As Mohamed left the pitch, both sets of fans stood up to clap his world-class performance, and the humble hero clapped right back.

At Basel, Mohamed had become a European star;

at Liverpool, he had become a European *super*star.
With two great goals and two amazing assists,
Mohamed had led Liverpool towards the Champions
League final, just as he had led his country, Egypt, to
the 2018 World Cup.

'So, just how good *is* Mohamed Salah?' the TV
presenter asked.

Liverpool legend Steven Gerrard smiled and replied:
'He's the best player on the planet right now!'

That had always been Mohamed's dream, ever
since he first kicked a football on his local pitch in
Nagrig.

SADIO MANÉ HONOURS

Red Bull Salzburg

🏆 Austrian Football Bundesliga: 2013–14

🏆 Austrian Cup: 2013–14

Liverpool

🏆 UEFA Champions League: 2018–19

Individual

🏆 CAF Team of the Year: 2015, 2016, 2018

🏆 PFA Premier League Team of the Year: 2016–17, 2018–19

🏆 Liverpool Players' Player of the Year: 2016–17

🏆 Liverpool Player of the Year: 2016–17

🏆 Premier League Golden Boot: 2018–19

MANE

10 **THE FACTS**

NAME: SADIO MANÉ

DATE OF BIRTH:
10 April 1992

AGE: 27

PLACE OF BIRTH:
Bambali, Sédhiou

NATIONALITY: Senegal

BEST FRIEND:
Kalidou Koulibaly

CURRENT CLUB: Liverpool

POSITION: LW

THE STATS

Height (cm):	175
Club appearances:	307
Club goals:	131
Club trophies:	3
International appearances:	60
International goals:	16
International trophies:	0
Ballon d'Ors:	0

  HERO RATING: 88

GREATEST MOMENTS

Type and search the web links to see the magic for yourself!

26 JULY 2012, GREAT BRITAIN 1–1 SENEGAL

https://www.youtube.com/watch?v=0PPeasuJsil
In 2012, Sadio helped lead Senegal to their first-ever Olympic Games. In their opening match in London, they took on Ryan Giggs's Great Britain. Sadio played brilliantly, but with ten minutes to go at Old Trafford, Senegal were losing 1–0. So, he dribbled forward down the right wing and split the GB defence with a beautiful through-ball to Moussa Konaté. 1–1!

2 18 JANUARY 2014, RB SALZBURG 3–0 BAYERN MUNICH

https://www.youtube.com/watch?v=ptDmL6eGq_w
This was only a midseason friendly, but Sadio didn't see it
that way. For him, it was a chance to show that he could
beat the big boys. Bayern Munich boss Pep Guardiola
put out a strong side, but Sadio destroyed them with his
amazing burst of speed. He scored the first goal himself
and then set up the other two for his teammates.

3 20 MARCH 2016, SOUTHAMPTON 3–2 LIVERPOOL

https://www.youtube.com/watch?v=dpIOf4Z9Atw
Sadio only came on for the second half of this Premier
League clash, and he completely changed the game.
Southampton were losing 2–0 at the time, but Sadio
quickly got his team back into the game. Then in the last
few minutes, he scored the winner to pull off an incredible
Saints comeback. The Liverpool defence couldn't cope
with him, but their manager Jürgen Klopp had a plan…

4
19 DECEMBER 2016,
EVERTON 0–1 LIVERPOOL

https://www.youtube.com/watch?v=zsAP-ca_TLE

This was the day that Sadio became a true Liverpool hero. In the dying seconds of the Merseyside derby, Daniel Sturridge's shot bounced back off the post. With a sudden burst of speed, Sadio reacted first and blasted the ball into the empty Everton net. 1–0 to Liverpool – what a moment to become a Merseyside Matchwinner!

5
14 FEBRUARY 2018,
PORTO 0–5 LIVERPOOL

https://www.youtube.com/watch?v=YYF4C_EAMzY

Sadio has scored lots of hat-tricks – including the fastest-ever in the Premier League – but this one in the Champions League quarter-finals is his favourite so far. His first two goals were nothing special but Sadio's third was a superstrike. With five minutes to go, the ball came to him just outside the penalty area. Sadio struck it beautifully, and it swerved past the Porto keeper.

PLAY LIKE YOUR HEROES

THE SADIO MANÉ 'BURST OF SPEED'

SEE IT HERE You Tube

https://www.youtube.com/watch?v=Iw0Lw_2D6CM

STEP 1: *ZOOM!* When you make your move, timing is everything. Go too early, and you'll be offside. Go too late, and the goalkeeper might get there first.

STEP 2: Make the *right* run. Point to where you want the pass to go and try to catch the defenders out by bursting in between them.

STEP 3: When you win the race to the through-ball, slow down and think. You'll need to stay calm and clever to score past the keeper.

STEP 4: But if the pass doesn't come to you, don't give up. Your teammates are world-class too! Get into the six-yard box, ready for any rebounds...

STEP 5: If the shot bounces off the post, react as quickly as you can. Race towards the ball and do whatever it takes to score – a sliding tap-in, a diving header etc.

TEST YOUR KNOWLEDGE

QUESTIONS

1. Who were Sadio's top two childhood football heroes?

2. Which country did Senegal beat in their first match at the 2002 World Cup?

3. Sadio watched the 2005 Champions League final on TV in Bambali – which teams were in it?

4. How old was Sadio when he made his brave journey to Senegal's capital city, Dakar?

5. Which future Senegal teammate did Sadio meet while playing for Metz?

6. Which international tournament in 2012 helped Sadio to make a name for himself?

7. What Premier League record did Sadio break at Southampton?

8. How much did Liverpool pay for Sadio, and what shirt number did he wear at first?

9. Sadio's Senegal qualified for the second round of the 2018 World Cup – true or false?

10. Who are the other two members of Liverpool's 'Big Three'?

11. How many Premier League goals did Sadio score in the 2018–19 season?

Answers below. . . No cheating!

1. *Ronaldinho and El-Hadji Diouf.* 2. *The reigning World Champions, France.* 3. *Liverpool & AC Milan* 4. *Fifteen* 5. *Kalidou Koulibaly* 6. *The Summer Olympics in London* 7. *He scored the fastest-ever hat-trick against Aston Villa – in two minutes and fifty-six seconds!* 8. *£34 million and Number 19* 9. *False – Japan went through instead because they got fewer yellow cards!* 10. *Mohamed Salah and Roberto Firmino* 11. *Twenty-two – he shared the Golden Boot with Mohamed.*